What Should I Do Now?

A Guide to Raising Children

What Should I Do Now?

A Guide to Raising Children

· by Wayne Rickerson ·

STANDARD PUBLISHING
Cincinnati, Ohio   29-03151

Contents

Introduction

It's not easy being a parent.

That is perhaps the understatement of the year. Being the parent of a child of any age is not easy; each age has its own set of difficulties and rewards. When your child is a preschooler he is underfoot most of the time. The energy drain is unbelievable. Things change when your child starts school. While your child is no longer underfoot during the day, you now have to deal with his growing independence. Others, such as teachers and friends, now have a growing influence on your child. It is an awesome task raising a school-age child. Much is at stake.

In this book I attempt to assist you in raising your children in two ways: First, I want you to know that your situation is shared by a multitude of other parents who have the same fears and frustrations. You are one of many who wonder just how good a job you are doing and whether your child is really going to be a well-adjusted Christian. Just knowing what to expect from yourself and your child can help you be a better parent. Second, I offer practical advice on how to guide your child through the formative years.

No book has all the answers for every parent. Each school-age child is unique. No two parents are the same. In this book I share with you some principles that Janet and I have found helpful in raising our children. Many times we have fallen short of the very principles we advocate in this book. We do not expect ourselves to be perfect parents and we hope that you do not expect too much from yourselves. We can, however, improve our skills as parents. God can help us make changes that will enable us to rear well-adjusted Christians.

You can use this book in four basic ways. First, you can read it yourself and answer the questions that follow each chapter. I strongly recommend you answer the questions, because they will cause you to probe deep into your own spirit. The questions will also help you make some decisions and apply what you are reading to your life.

A second way of using this book is to read the book together with your spouse and answer the questions at the end of each chapter separately. (You will find that there are two sets of questions for each chapter.) Take some time for just the two of you to discuss the answers to your questions. Make some decision together on how you will handle your child.

A third way to use this book is in a 13-week course format. I have written a Leader's Guide that gives a simple, practical approach for teaching the concepts in this book. You can use this Leader's Guide in a Bible-school class, Sunday evening or weeknight electives, or as an aid to parenting groups.

A fourth way to use this book is in a small parenting group. I recommend forming small groups of not more than ten parents of school age children to meet weekly and discuss the material in this book. The discussion questions at the end of each chapter are designed for group use. By sharing with other parents, we receive encouragement and support and we learn from one another.

How to Form Parenting Groups

The plan is simple. First you elect a group leader or leaders, depending on how many groups you want to form. I suggest using couples when possible. The couple ideally should be one who has raised or is raising school-age children and has done an effective job with them. That is not to say they should be "perfect parents." *There is no such species.* Such a person, if he existed, would be ill-fitted to deal with the rest of us mortal parents who make a few too many mistakes. The leaders should be persons who are willing to share their defeats as well as their victories.

Next you find a group of parents who would like to develop some insights into guiding school-age children. *There are a lot of such people around.* There should be a minimum of five and a maximum of twelve parents in your group.

Next you decide what schedule fits your church program. If you have existing family groups that meet regularly and are age-graded, then I suggest you use these existing groups and times. If you do not have this situation then you will need to form separate parenting groups. It works well to have these groups meet in homes.

This book is divided into three sections of four, four and five chapters each. Unless the group is meeting during the Bible-school hour, it is best to have the parenting groups meet for shorter times rather than the full thirteen sessions.

If you choose the small-group format, I suggest you run your first group for four weeks, covering the basic material in the section, *Building Foundations.* At the end of this time, ask the group if they would like to set a time to study the next section on *Basics of Parenting.* If they choose to meet again you can again find the interest level for the final section, *What to Do When Your Children Fight.*

How to Lead a Parenting Group

The group sessions are very simple. Each couple or person gets a book. Before the group session, everyone reads the chapter and answers the questions at the end of the chapter. The group leaders (a husband/wife team, if possible) answers the same questions. The group then shares the answers to their questions as the group leader guides the conversation. I suggest one-to two-hour sessions.

It is generally a good rule to start with question one, because it is designed to be an "opener" to the general topic. There is no way you will cover all the questions in one hour. It is possible in two hours. The purpose of the questions is to help parents look into their own lives and make some personal applications. Not all of this has to be shared with the group. *Choose the questions that you feel are important for your group to cover.*

Several ingredients make parenting groups effective. Encouragement and support are vital. Another important element is input. Parents receive their initial input by reading the chapters. More input comes from the other parents during the sessions. Introspection is also necessary. Introspection occurs as individuals answer the questions at the end of each chapter. This causes them to examine themselves.

Sharing is a very important part of the process. Through sharing, I hear myself. As I verbalize I can start putting my own problems into perspective. I get insights into myself and my parenting problems. You have probably had that experience already. You have a problem and you ask a friend to help you solve it. You start talking and by the time you're finished you thank your friend for helping you solve your problem. He says, "I didn't say a word!" By verbalizing your problem to someone who cared, you were able to solve it your own problem.

A final ingredient that will make your parenting group effective is application. The last question on every discussion page asks the parent to commit himself to some kind of specific plan to change. This is essential. Simply knowing facts or Biblical insights will not insure growth. Only when we *apply* those principles to our lives will real growth occur.

At the end of your parenting sessions, suggest that couples go home and decide together on what changes need to be made within their homes.

One last word of encouragement—Janet and I are excited about the opportunity God has given us to *grow with our children.* Through the pain and frustrations, we have seen God's hand building maturity in our own lives. While there is no denying the anxieties that accompany raising children, there can be a great deal of joy as we see our children mature. *I am glad that God gave me the opportunity to be a parent.* May God bless your pilgrimage through this book!

Section 1

Building Foundations

CHAPTER 1

It Sounded Too Simple

You've been calling him your "big boy," but as your six-year-old struts off for his first day of school, he doesn't seem so big. In fact, he seems awfully small and vulnerable as he walks out the door, lunch in hand. You get a knot in your stomach as your child enters a new world, the world of the school-age child. You've tried to prepare him for this day, but now you are not so sure you've done an adequate job. How can a six-year-old child survive the traumas of school—difficult skills to learn, taunting by peers, non-Christian influences, and even the possibility of an insensitive teacher?

Even though you've been preparing your child and yourself for this inevitable day, it is not easy. Your child will now be spending a large proportion of his day away from your influence, out of your control. You now have to trust the character that you, God, and your child have been working together to develop. You will have to entrust some of his development to others.

I have just described a few of the many emotions associated with raising children. Nothing really can prepare us adequately for the emotions of being a parent.

It sounded so simple: Get married, have children, rear bright successful children—enjoy grandchildren. But now we know different. Raising children is joy, frustration, pain, delight and just plain hard work.

The following is a list of some feelings I see many parents experiencing. Make a check mark next to the ones that you identify with. Make a star next to the most dominant emotions you are feeling right now.

I feel, sometimes, that I was never cut out to be a parent.

I feel, sometimes, that my spouse and I disagree about so many expectations for our children, it may harm them.

I feel that our children have so many outside negative influences that I wonder if they will remain true to God.

I feel that I don't have enough knowledge about rearing children to be a good parent.

I feel, sometimes, that I am losing control of my children.

I sometimes experience strong negative emotions toward my children that cause me to feel severe guilt.

If you checked two or more of the previous statements, welcome to the "Normal Parents Club." If you check less than two statements, then you have passed the course . . . read no further.

Most of us experience some of the feelings I have just described. Many of these feelings are normal. However, if these feelings are frequent and severe, controlling our lives, then some changes need to be made. Parents are probably as unsure of themselves today as any time in the history of our nation. It hasn't been too many years ago that parents seemed confident in raising their children. Families were not as mobile in those days. Parents could find all the support they needed from relatives and friends that lived nearby. Mothers, fathers, aunts and uncles assured new parents that if they would abide by the basics of child rearing (strong love, strong discipline), everything would turn out all right.

Today with the mobility of families, the demise of the extended family, the confusion of values, and diverse child-rearing philosophies, parents are unsure of themselves. I believe God wants Christian parents to be confident. Confidence comes from a deep trust in God, a strong belief in the wisdom God is developing in you, and the development of some basic parenting skills. I hope as a result of reading this book, you will deepen your trust in God, come to believe that you are already a much better parent than you sometimes feel, and develop some skills to help you become an even better parent.

Three Priorities of Family Life

Three priorities are essential for building a successful Christian family. These are (1) a vital relationship with God, (2) a vital relationship with your spouse, and (3) a vital relationship with your children.

Priority 1: A Vital Relationship With God

The first and most vital relationship is with God. This is the foundation of all other relationships. If we have a vital love relationship with God, then we are in a position to have a vital relationship with our family. Jesus implied this order of priorities when answering the lawyer's question, "Which is the great commandment in the Law?" Jesus answered, "You shall love the Lord your God with all your heart, and with all your soul, and with all your mind. This is the great and foremost commandment. And a second is like it, You shall love your neighbor as yourself. On these two commandments depend the whole Law and the Prophets" (Matthew 22:36-40).

All family relationships are based on the quality of your relationship with God. This starts when you are born into the family of God through placing your trust in Jesus. This is only the beginning. We are born into the family of God as babes, but we are expected to grow toward maturity in Christ. God has given us food that never fails to produce maturity, His Word. A daily diet of His Word gives us growth necessary for other vital relationships in our life. Second Timothy 3:16, 17 says, "All Scripture is inspired by God and profitable for teaching, for reproof, for correction, for training in righteousness; that the man of God may be adequate, equipped for every good work."

God's Word will equip us for the "good work" of parenting. God's Word will build in us the character needed to become effective parents. We all have areas of our personality that hinder us in parenting. Mine is a quick temper and lack of a gentle spirit. Through "the sword of the Spirit, which is the Word of God" (Ephesians 6:17), God is working to slow my temper and build a gentle spirit in me.

A daily diet of God's Word is an absolute necessity for me to be an effective parent. When I do not take enough time with the Lord each day, in the reading of God's Word, memorization, meditation, and prayer, I can tell the difference in my family relationships. The quick temper starts raising its ugly horns. The motivation for a gentle spirit starts to fade away.

I urge you to start a daily quiet time with the Lord, if you do not have one. If your quiet time lacks direction, here is a suggestion for a format.

Reading God's Word. Get a notebook with blank pages. Start with a book of the Bible and read a passage each day. Ask yourself the following questions about the passage: (1) What does this passage tell me about God? (2) What does this passage say to me? (3) What does God want me to do?

Write out your answers. This helps you to apply God's Word to your life. It is not what we know that is important, but how we apply what we know to our lives. God's Word is to be "lived out."

Memorization and meditation. Start by memorizing just one or two verses a week. Meditate on the verse. Meditation is visualizing the verses, mulling them over in your mind and applying them to your life. Your greatest spiritual growth will come from memorization and meditation.

Prayer. Write down specific prayer requests and then record God's answers. Pray for your children every day. I suggest praying together as a couple. Janet and I have done this and feel it brings great strength to our marriage.

Priority 2: A Vital Relationship With Your Spouse

As a Christian parent, your highest priority is your relationship with God. Close behind, in second place, is your relationship with your spouse. The climate of your marriage directly effects your children. No amount of good parenting skills can compensate for a poor marriage relationship. *Our focus needs to be on one another, not our children.* I had to learn this the hard way. I have always been very child-centered. It was very easy for me, in the early years of our marriage, to spend quality time developing a good relationship with the three girls. I often wondered why Janet seemed to resent the time I spent with them. After all, wasn't I pleasing her by being an outstanding father? I also wondered why our marriage relationship was not what it should be.

God convicted me that I had my priorities out of place. I had actually placed the children above my wife. I repented of this sin in my life and asked forgiveness from my wife. I committed myself to making her my second highest priority, after my relationship with God. As a result, we have a close, growing marriage and the children have benefited.

> Our whole relationship with our children is going to be different, if we focus on our spouse rather than on our children. Sometimes we think that the more attention we pay directly to our children, the more they are going to feel loved and appreciated. Actually, the more absorbed that we are with one another, and the more the children continue to get their meaning from our relationship with one another, the more they are going to have.[1]

We all come into our marriage with a certain amount of brokenness. By "brokenness" I mean spiritual and emotional weaknesses such as poor self-image, anger, lack of patience, and memories from our own families that warp the way we think and act around our own children. This brokenness interferes with our parenting skills and our relationship with our children. Besides, we sometimes pass

19

that brokenness on to our children for them to deal with in *their* families. I believe that this is part of the meaning of the Scripture that says, "He will by no means leave the guilty unpunished, visiting the iniquity of fathers on the children and on the grandchildren to the third and fourth generations" (Exodus 34:7).

When we have a close, intimate marriage, I believe God has a way of diffusing that individual brokenness that we bring into a marriage. We merge our strengths and weaknesses into "one flesh" (Genesis 2:24) We complete one another; we refine one another. Through the strength of oneness, our children receive more of our strengths than our weaknesses.

Children do not always contribute to marital harmony. There have been times when our children have brought stress into our marriage. Sometimes Janet and I disagree on expectations for the children. When things are going poorly with the children, it is a great temptation to blame one another for what's going on. During these stressful periods, we have stopped several times and agreed, *we are not going to let problems with our children damage our marriage relationship.* We are committed to working toward unity. "Problems with children have as great a potential to strengthen a marriage as to wreck it. They can bring you together in a new unity or blow you apart."[2]

Figure 1-1 illustrates the effect that children have on marital satisfaction.[3]

One of the greatest dangers facing couples today is the problem of the parallel marriage. Many couples are living parallel lives. It is amazing how the pressures of having young children at home, combined with making a living and busy schedules, can create separate lives for husbands and wives. It is easy for a husband and wife to become parallel to one another. By "parallel" I mean two people livng in the same house but very seldom doing things together or having meaningful communication.

A study in *Redbook* magazine illustrates the problem of the parallel marriage in many marriages today. *Redbook* surveyed over 700 marriage counselors on the ten most common problems facing couples today. Number one was communication. Number two was, "The loss of shared

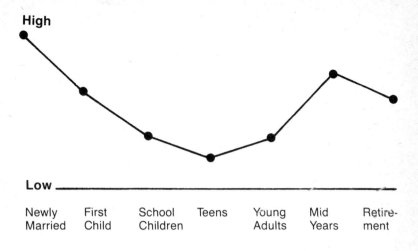

High

Low | Newly Married | First Child | School Children | Teens | Young Adults | Mid Years | Retire- ment

Figure 1-1. Level of Marital Satisfaction

goals and interests," and number five was, "The fun and excitement has gone out of marriage."

Do not let anything stand in the way of your relationship with one another. You need quality time for just the two of you each week. Janet and I have what we call our "Together Time." This is a time away from the children for just the two of us to talk, look at our schedules, plan, and resolve issues. This is one way we guard against the parallel marriage. Our Together Time reminds us each week that we have committed ourselves to growing closer to God and to one another. When our children were young we would put them to bed and have Together Time later in the evening. Now our schedule allows us to meet at noon. Try having a weekly Together Time. I believe it will bring real strength to your marriage.

> I cannot exaggerate the importance of parental harmony. Children need it, and need it more than ever when they go wrong. Their well-being depends on it. The welfare of the children rests more on parental unity than on any child-rearing expertise the parents may have. Parents can get away with many mistakes if their children see them as a solid, loving alliance. Such an alliance creates a context in which children can respond with respect and obedience.[4]

Priority 3: A Vital Relationship
With Our Children

When we have committed ourselves to a vital relationship with God and a vital relationship with our spouse, the stage is set for a vital relationship with our children. This is the third in the order of Biblical priorities, but it is certainly not unimportant. Psalms says that "children are a gift of the Lord." Any gift from God is important. This gift needs to be handled with the utmost care.

Three phases of a parent-child relationship. It is important for you to understand the three phases of a parent-child relationship. The first stage is "Bonding." During the early years of our child's life we go through this very important stage. As loving parents we build a close relationship with our children. We meet their physical needs. We meet their emotional needs by giving them emotional support and physical affection. By our actions our children feel secure and loved within the family circle. We are in control. They are dependent upon us for their existence.

The second phase is "Debonding." During the teenage years our children must debond from us by moving from dependence to independence. Debonding takes place as our teens pull back emotionally from us. They demand more time by themselves—with friends. They argue against our "old-fashioned standards." Their speech and dress all indicate that they are in the process of debonding.

The third phase of the parent-child relationship is "Rebonding." After your teenager leaves home a natural rebonding occurs. He now has a well-established identity, is independent, and no longer feels it necessary to pull away from you. The task is now completed and a new, warm, mature relationship emerges.

You are now in the important "Bonding" phase with your young child. The quality of the relationship you build with him now will affect the rest of his life.

This phase of parenting will be successful if you decide now to have a vital relationship with your child. I decided when Heidi was born that I would work diligently to have a vital relationship with her and any other children we might have. It has taken time and energy over the past 22 years, but it has been worth the effort. It has meant sacrificing some things that I have wanted to do over the years. It has meant laying down books and newspapers to play games. It has meant playing hide and seek, walking to the zoo, playing fort under tables, making houses out of cardboard boxes, and other "exciting" ventures. It has meant listening when I really wasn't interested. It has meant once-a-week special times with the children over a period of years. Those early years of "bonding" have been worth every minute invested. Heidi has just graduated from college, Liesl is married and has her first child, and Bridget is a senior in high school. The early bonding made a significant contribution to the excellent relationships we now enjoy with our three children.

Keith Leenhouts, in one of the finest books on parent-child relationships ever written, tells about an incident with his son that sums up what commitment to building a vital relationship with your children is all about.

Another year of duties, obligations, and sacrifices passed. Instead of going to Friday night high-school football games with my friends, Bill and I stood on the railroad tracks overlooking the gridiron where I spent half my time watching him build imaginary fires and half my time watching the game. I gave up golf to spend Saturday and Sunday afternoons with him. And I tried not to stay up so late on weekend nights that I would be too tired the next day to play with him.

I accepted all these sacrifices and more, not because I particularly wanted to, but because I felt I should. This never truly bothered me, however, for I had always believed that true happiness is found in the fulfillment of duties, not in the pursuit of joys.

Then, on a bitterly cold January day when Bill was five, I unexpectedly discovered that fatherhood is not duties, obligations, and sacrificies, but a great joy. That entire Saturday afternoon I tried to help Bill learn to use single-bladed skates on a neighbor's frozen backyard swimming pool. All afternoon Bill tried and failed to skate the full length of the pool. Finally, with red cheeks taut with determination, and with staccato puffs of steamy breath shooting through the wool scarf that covered his mouth, he skated all the way across. He made it!

Well, I should say, part of him made it. Just before he reached his goal, the end of the pool, he tripped and smacked his nose on the edge. I skated over, picked him up, and said elatedly, "You made it, Bill! That was really great!"

But rubbing his nose and looking at the bright red blood staining the snow on his mittens, he looked up at me through tears and sniffed, "I—I didn't think it was so great."

I began to laugh, not so much because of what he had said and done, but because suddenly, standing there on my ice skates, wiping blood from the nose of our five-year-old son, I realized I was with Bill because I loved him and would rather be with him than with anyone else in the entire world, except, of course, his mother.

What a beautiful moment! I no longer felt I was "giving up something." I was receiving an experience of myself that had released a new potential for loving. Fatherhood was no longer just a duty—it had just become one of the greatest experiences I would ever know."[5]

No perfect parent. Just a final word about what to expect from yourself as a parent. There are no perfect parents. And it's a good thing. If we were perfect parents, our children would be ill-prepared for life in an imperfect world. In fact if we can do just half of what we know, half of the time we are excelling in parenthood. There are lots of ideals in this book. We need to work towards ideals, but let's go easy on ourselves. Trying to be "the perfect parent" will only weigh us down to where parenting becomes a drudgery.

Both you and your child have a responsibility to God. You have a responsibility to be the best parent possible. Your child has a responsibility to God to respond to your parenting. No one can help someone who doesn't want to be helped. The Scriptures say, "It is by his deeds that a lad distinguishes himself if his conduct is pure and right" (Proverbs 20:11).

God does not want us to take total responsibility for either our children's achievements or failures. To do so would deny both God's activity in their lives and their free will to choose.

All God expects of us is to commit ourselves sacrifically to the task of parenting. Feelings of inadequacy and low self-esteem will visit us occasionally. When problems and conflict occur, we must acknowledge our child's responsibility and God's influence in his life.

[1]Chuck Gallagher, *Parents Are Lovers*. New York: Doubleday, 1977. p. 105.

[2]John White, *Parents in Pain* (Downers Grove, IL: InterVarsity Press, 1979. p. 105.

[3]Jan Aldous, *Family Careers—Developmental Change in Families.*

[4]White, p. 106.

[5]Keith J. Leenhouts, *A Father ... A Son ... and a Three Mile Run.* Grand Rapids, MI: Zondervan Publishing House, 1975. pp. 33, 34.

Discussion Questions

1. Every parent has strengths and weaknesses. Give a strength you have as a parent.

2. The author lists six emotions that parents often experience. Which emotion affects you the most?

3. Share what you feel is the greatest obstacle in raising a child in today's society.

4. The author states that our relationship with God directly affects our relationship with our children. Tell why you believe this to be right or wrong.

5. Evaluate your "quiet time" with the Lord by circling one of the following:
   I have a vital quiet time.
   I need to improve my quiet time.
   I need to commit myself to a quiet time.

6. What are some possible consequences of parenting when a couple does not have their marriage as the number two priority?

7. What "brokenness" has God diffused in your marriage because of "oneness?"

8. In what ways is your marriage a "parallel" marriage?

9. What emotions did you experience when you read Keith Leenhouts' story about his son?

10. After reading this chapter and evaluating myself, one thing I will change to improve my parenting is ...

CHAPTER 2

Teaching Christian Values in the Family

If I were to ask you, "What Christian value would you most like your children to learn?" what would you say? I have asked this question to parents in seminars for the last 15 years. Their answers all center around the value of their children having a vital relationship with God.

As Christian parents we are deeply concerned about providing an environment where our children will learn a set of Christian values that will enable them to live a successful Christian life. The question is how can we teach Christian values in the midst of a pagan culture. Every day our children are exposed to the world's values. These values are taught by the TV, music, and at school by their peers.

The Battle of Values

Throughout history there has always been a battle between God's values and the values of man. Christ brought a new value system to the world. It was in constant conflict with religious people of His day. You will face this same battle in your family. Your children will hear and see your value system and at the same time be exposed to the world's value system. The good news is that God has equipped us for the battle. We have the power of His Word and His Spirit that can shape the values of our children. We can trust that the power of God is greater than the power of the world.

What Are Your Values?

What are your values? What values would you most like to pass on to your children? In Figure 2-1 below, make a list of the ten Christian values you would most like to pass on to your children. But first let me define a "Christian value." A Christian value is something that God thinks is important. A non-Christian value is something that the world thinks is important and is in opposition to God's values. Christian values include such things as character qualities: patience, love, endurance, trust, prayer, worship, love of God, witnessing, etc.

In the exercise there is a place to write Scriptures that correspond to your values and a place to evaluate how well you are living out that value in your own life.

Value	Scriptures	How well do I live out this value?
1.		
2.		
3.		
4.		
5.		
6.		
7.		
8.		
9.		
10.		

Figure 2-1. Christian Values You Want to Teach

If you are like most parents, this exercise has been very difficult for you. We all have value systems but seldom do we really think about what they are and more specifically, which values we would like our children to learn.

The Perfect Plan—
How We Are Taught Christian Values by God

How are we to teach these Christian values to our children? Let's take a look at the perfect plan—how God teaches Christian values to us. In Figure 2-2 you will see that we are born into this relationship with our heavenly Father. It is after we are born into this relationship that God begins to teach us His values. It is because of God's love for us that we are motivated to live out His values (2 Corinthians 5:14, 15). The qualities of God's love that produce a teachable spirit in us are listed.

The Perfect Plan—Imperfect Parents

God has given us the perfect plan, but we are not perfect parents. While we can never be the perfect teacher that God is because of His perfect love, we can grow in these qualities of love. Our children are born into a loving relationship with us. The living out of these qualities maintains that relationship, which produces a teachable spirit in our children. Rate yourself in the qualities of love given in Figure 2-2. Place a star by your strongest quality, and a check by the quality in which you need the most work.

God's Curriculum for the Home

God has not only given us an example of how to teach our children, but also of what we are to teach them. I believe that God's curriculum for the home was given by Jesus: "Love the Lord your God with all your heart, and with all your soul, and with all your mind.... Love your neighbor as yourself" (Matthew 22:37-39).

Every Christian value that you teach your children will fall under one of the three areas listed in these verse. Love of God and love of others are the two great values of the Christian faith. Almost everything we teach our children will involve ways of living out these two great values. The third area is implied in this Scripture passage, and that is to have an *appropriate* love for ourselves. We are to love our neighbor as ourself. God expects us to have healthy self-esteem because of His great love for us. It is important for us to teach the value of self-esteem to our children, for without it they will have difficulty loving others.

New Birth—Father

Born into God's family and a loving relationship with our heavenly Father.

Qualities of the loving relationship that provide the desire for us to be taught:

Unconditional Love (1 John 4:16; Psalm 89:1, 2; 1 John 5:11-13)
Compassion (Psalm 103:13)
Knows Us Completely (Psalm 139:1-3)
Accepts Our Limitations (Psalm 103:14)
Always Has Time for Us (Psalm 34:4)
Meets Our Basic Needs (Matthew 7:11)
Is Righteous (Psalm 11:7)
Disciplines Us in Love (Hebrews 12:4-6)

This Love Produces . . . Teachable Spirit
(2 Corinthians 5:14, 15)

Father

Natural Birth—Family

Our children are born into a loving relationship with us.

Family

As parents, we must live out the qualities of the loving relationship that produces a desire in our child to be taught.

Rate yourself on scale of 1-10:

	low				medium				high	
Unconditional Love	1	2	3	4	5	6	7	8	9	10
Compassion	1	2	3	4	5	6	7	8	9	10
Knowing Your Child	1	2	3	4	5	6	7	8	9	10
Accepting Your Child	1	2	3	4	5	6	7	8	9	10
Time for Your Child	1	2	3	4	5	6	7	8	9	10
Meeting Your Child's Needs	1	2	3	4	5	6	7	8	9	10
Maturity in Christ	1	2	3	4	5	6	7	8	9	10
Discipline Child in Love	1	2	3	4	5	6	7	8	9	10

This Love Produces . . . Teachable Spirit

Figure 2-2. The Perfect Plan—How We Are Taught Christian Values

List some values you could teach your children in each of these areas.

God's Curriculum (Matthew 22:37-39)

Love of God   Love of Others   Love of Self

Methods for Teaching Christian Values in the Family

Three methods are extremely helpful when teaching Christian values to our children. These three methods were given by God, through Moses, to the children of Israel before they inherited the promised land.

> Hear, O Israel! The Lord is our God, the Lord is one! And you shall love the Lord your God with all your heart and with all your soul and with all your might. And these words, which I am commanding you today, shall be on your heart; and you shall teach them diligently to your sons and shall talk of them when you sit in your house and when you walk by the way and when you lie down and when you rise up. And you shall bind them as a sign on your hand and they shall be as frontals on your forehead. And you shall write them on the doorposts of your house and on your gates (Deuteronomy 6:4-9).

The understanding of this Scripture passage has been greatly enhanced by Howard Hendricks, professor of Christian Education and Leadership Development at Dallas Theological Seminary. Dr. Hendricks, a strong advocate of parents teaching Christian values in the family, sees three vital methods coming from Scripture. Modeling, or teaching by example; talk, or informal teaching; and structured teaching.

First, parents were to teach by example. Parents were to have God's laws in their own hearts first and *then* teach them to their children. This is extremely important. Like myself, you have probably tried to teach your children something that you were not practicing yourself. It just does not work. Children believe and often learn what they see, not what is told to them, unless the two mesh. Our task as teachers is to become godly examples to our children. They will learn primarily from our modeling.

A second method found in this passage is "talk," or informal teaching. Parents were to talk of God's laws to their children. This means verbalizing our faith to our children in the everyday routine of our lives. This includes looking for the "teachable" moment in your children's lives. "Talking" involves applying God's Word to everything we do.

A third principle involves structured teaching, or a time set aside by parents to teach specific Christian values. The word "impress" in the Hebrew infers this kind of teaching. This is perhaps the most difficult for us to accomplish. For some reason, family devotions, family nights, and other kinds of more formal teaching, are a threat. In the next chapter I will show you some ways to teach Christian values in a more structured setting and have fun with your children at the same time.

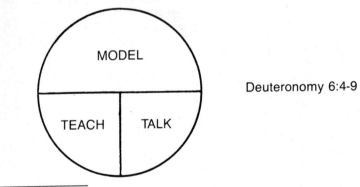

Deuteronomy 6:4-9

Figure 2-3. Model, Teach, Talk

So there we have it—the Model, Talk, and Teach of communicating Christian values. This can become a teaching lifestyle for us. These methods of teaching Christian values can help us become effective transmitters of the faith to our children.

Conclusion

God has made us, as parents, primarily responsible to teach Christian values to our children. He has shown us the perfect plan by the way He teaches us. He has given us a core curriculum and methods for teaching that curriculum.

God will bless our efforts to teach our children. We can always trust that what God expects of us, He also enables. God will enable you to effectively teach Christian values to your children.

Discussion Questions

1. What Christian value would you most like your children to learn?

2. On page 28, list the ten values you would like to pass on to your children. What was this experience like for you?

3. Rate yourself on the qualities of love listed on page 30. What are your strengths? What are your weaknesses?

4. What quality of love would you most like to develop in your life right now?

5. Which quality of God's love do you appreciate most?

6. Read Matthew 22:37-39. Which of the three loves is the most difficult for you to live out in your own life? Why?

7. List at least two values that you would like to teach your children in the three "God's curriculum" columns on page 31.

8. Which of the three methods for teaching Christian values in the family is the easiest for you to use? Which is the most difficult?

9. Can you think of an example of a value that you are trying to teach your children that is being contradicted by your modeling?

10. What one thing will you do to more effectively teach Christian values to your children?

CHAPTER 3

Building Family Togetherness— Family Times That Work

The family of the 80's finds it increasingly difficult to set aside quality family time. Most parents want to build family togetherness through time together but have difficulty finding the time and energy and then deciding what to do.

These are some of the same dilemmas Janet and I faced with our young family some years ago. We made some decisions we will never regret. Although I was a busy pastor, we decided to make family time a priority. One of the most successful ways we did this was to have a once-a-week Family Night. I still believe that this is a good answer for busy families. Over the years we faithfully used Wednesday evening to play games, learn Biblical principles and have fun. I believe that regular family times helped us build those special relationships as a family that are still evident today with our 17-, 21-, and 22-year-old children. The kind of family times I am referring to are regular times of fun and fellowship based on Biblical principles.

First I want to give you some guidelines that will help you have successful family times. Second, I will give some family time ideas that you can use with your family right away.

Guidelines for Successful Family Times

1. *Make a commitment to have regular family times.* Once the commitment is made it is much easier to arrange other things around the time you have scheduled for your family.

2. *Find ideas that will help make your time together enjoyable.* I would like to suggest several resources for successful family times. Dean and Grace Merrill have written an excellent book titled *Together At Home* (Thomas Nelson, publishers). I have written the following family time resource books: *Christian Family Activities for Families With Preschoolers, Christian Family Activities for Families With School Age Children* and *Christian Family Activities for Families With Teens.* Each of the books have about a year's supply of activities if used once a week. The activities are built around the teaching of Biblical principles. The most recent book I have written is titled *Family Fun Times.* All four of these books are published by Standard Publishing.

3. *Let everyone in the family participate.* One of the most important principles in successful family times is to make leadership a family affair. Let one of your children lead in prayer, another lead the game, another serve dessert, etc.

4. *Have fun.* The most important guideline is to have fun. The resources I have mentioned have teaching, but teaching within the family works best when everyone is having a good time. Children learn through play. Concentrate on having fun, and your family times will be a success.

Family Time Plans

To help you get started, I suggest you try family times for the next four weeks. Read through the following family time plans. Each plan contains more ideas than you will want to use on a single family night. Don't try to use all the activities in each plan. *Select only the ones that you feel your family will enjoy and ignore the others.* Remember, pass around the responsibilities. Make sure everyone in the family has something to do. Have fun, and don't forget that special dessert. I suspect that at the end of the four weeks, family night will be a permanent part of your family life.

Family Time One—
What Makes a House a Home?

Goal: The goal of this family night is to help family members appreciate your home and encourage them to express this appreciation by doing at least one thing to make your home a happier place to live.

For parents: We rarely take time as a family to think of the many beautiful ways in which God helps us make our house a home. Someday our children will reflect upon their home and relive memories that we are building now. What will they think of? Will they have warm memories from which to draw strength in later years?

God, the master builder, wants to use us, His carpenters, to build beautiful Christian homes. Family times can be a useful tool for building memories in the home. Use this family time to think together on "What Makes a House a Home?"

1. *The home happening.* Mom and Dad should start this family time by describing the house or houses in which they spent their childhood. Describe not only what the house looked like but also what made those houses happy homes to live in.

Give each family member a house cutout as shown below. Have him write under the doors and windows what he feels makes a house a home.

Prepare these house cutouts in advance for your family. Use one sheet of construction paper for each. Cut out a large house (approximately 6″ x 8″) similar to the one shown in Figure 3-1. Cut the two windows and one door so that they will open. Trace the house you have just cut out on a plain piece of white typing paper, then glue the paper to the back of the construction paper house. Now each window and the door has paper behind it to write on.

Have each person, in turn, open the windows and door

37

on his or her house and write or draw what makes a house a home.

Discuss how loving God, loving one another, doing things together, being considerate of each other, and sharing God's Word together help make a house a home.

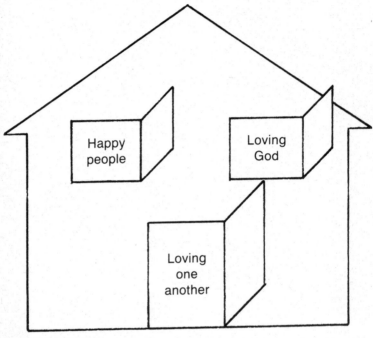

Figure 3-1. The Home Happening

2. *Who builds the home?* Read Psalm 127 and discuss the following questions.

—Who builds the home?
—In what ways does God build our home?
—How can God use parents to build a happy home?
—How can God use children to build a happy home?

Have each person list two ways in which he can be used by God to build a happy home. Share these with one another.

Challenge family members to turn their ideas into personal goals that will help make the home a happier place to live.

3. *Finish the sentences.* The following open-ended sentences will help family members express their feelings about your home. Have each one, in turn, finish the sentences out loud.
   —My home makes me feel ...
   —The thing I like best about my home is ...
   —When I am away from home, the thing I miss
      most is ...
   —My best memory about home is ...
   —I wish our home could be more ...
   —One thing I could do to make our home a happier
      place to live is ...

4. *The grand tour.* Take a tour of your house. Go into every room and have each person think of some way he can help make it a happy room. Some things that could be done are: help keep the bathroom clean, keep the bedroom clean, pick up in the living room, and wash the dishes. Remember that the family working together makes a house a happy home.

5. *Treasure hunt.* Cut out five three-inch-high houses on which to write the clues to the treasure. Plant the clues in various rooms of the house. Have the final clue lead to the kitchen. The treasure should be a special snack that you have ready for your family.

6. *For families with teens.* This activity will help you get better acquainted as you think about one another and your home. Every home has a "family personality"—a composite of the values and interests of the occupants. However, if one person were to design a home only for himself, it would reflect his personality.

Have each person choose another family member for whom to design a home. This home should reflect that person's interests and personality. You may either sketch the house or write a short paragraph describing what this person's house would be like. Be specific. What kind of furniture would he prefer? What colors would he use? What hobbies or interests would be in evidence?

When this project is done, ask the person for whom you planned the house how close it is to being accurate. Then as a family, discuss the following:

—In what ways does our home reflect the personalities of the various family members?
—What are some things that make our house a home?
—What do you like best about our home?
—What changes will you make in your own home?
—How can our home be improved?

Have each person think of one thing he will do to make your home a happier place to live.

7. *For families with young children.* With a little adapting, the Home Happening, Grand Tour, and Treasure Hunt activities will work well with young children.

Another activity you might enjoy is to play house with your little children. Select some dress-up clothes. Let the little ones be the mother and father and you the children. Have this activity lead you into a discussion of the following questions:

—What makes a happy home?
—How does loving God help make a happy home?
—How does loving one another help make a happy home?
—How does helping mother and father help make a happy home?
—How does obeying help make a happy home?
—How does doing things together help make a happy home?

Have each child think of one thing he will do to help make your home happy.

Family Time Two—
Caring for Personal Possessions

Goal: This family time is to help family members become more sensitive to others' feelings about personal possessions and to develop some guidelines for respecting the rights of others in the family.

For parents: Lack of respect for personal property within the home is a problem in many families. One reason for this recurring problem is that children have difficulty identifying with the feelings of others. This is caused, in part, by their limited conceptual development. They have problems putting themselves in the place of others.

This family night is designed to help your children become more sensitive toward other people's feelings about personal possessions. Select the activities you think your children will appreciate.

1. *My most prized possession.* Have each person conceal his most prized personal possession and bring it to the family circle. If the possession is too large to hide, it may be left in its place until later in the activity.

Family members must guess what everyone's personal possession is by asking each person not more than ten yes-or-no questions about that possession. Go around the family circle with each person asking one question until the possession has been discovered or the 10 questions have been asked. The person being questioned must then show his possession and tell why he chose it.

Use this procedure until all family members have shown their prized possessions.

Discuss: How do you feel when someone mistreats your possessions? What other personal possessions should be respected? (mail, clothes, jewelry, etc.)

2. *Unscramble the verse.* Each house below contains a word of a very special Scripture verse: "Treat others as you want them to treat you" (Luke 6:31, Living Bible). Unscramble each word and place the words in proper order to discover the verse.

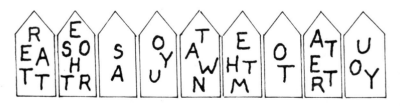

Figure 3-2. Unscramble the Verse

Discuss: How can this verse help us respect other family members' personal possessions? What changes must we make in our actions?

Now give each person five minutes (more or less, depending on the ages of your children) to study the verse. When the verse has been memorized, say the first word of the verse and go around the family circle with each person adding a word until it is completed. If someone misses a word, start over.

3. *Picture the verse.* Give everyone a piece of paper and crayons or marking pens and have him draw a picture that illustrates the principle of Luke 6:31. This could be a picture of a family member showing respect for another's personal possessions. When all family members have completed them, show and discuss these pictures.

4. *Role play.* Have two of your children role play the following situations: One child is sitting in his room studying. Another child charges into the room, takes something without asking and walks out. Tell your children to act out the roles in their own ways. They are free to use whatever gestures or conversation they feel is appropriate.

Stop role play before a solution is reached and discuss what happened. Who was at fault? What rights were violated? How did the other person respond? What could have prevented the unhappy situation?

Now have your children role play the same situation again, this time being considerate for one another's personal rights and possessions. Discuss the difference between attitudes represented by the role plays.

5. *The untouchables.* Have each family member make a list of personal possessions he wishes others would not touch without permission. Next have everyone take a new piece of paper and write each family member's name on it. Beside each name he should list that person's "untouchables." Each person should keep his list to remind him of the importance of respecting other family members' personal possessions.

6. *Personal possessions and sharing.* There is always the danger of becoming selfish with our personal possessions. We need to remember that all we have comes from God. There is a delicate balance between protecting personal possessions and sharing with others. To help clarify this balance discuss the following questions:
—When should we be willing to share our personal possessions?
—Are there times when we should not share our personal possessions?
—Read Luke 6:31 and Matthew 22:39. What principles do these verses contain that can help us know when and what to share?

7. *Personal possession policy.* On the basis of the Scriptures you have read and your discussion, formulate a one-sentence policy for your family about personal possessions.

Have each family member write this policy on an index card and keep it in his room as a guide to solving the sticky problems concerning personal possessions.

8. *For families with teens:* Adolescents have very strong feelings about their rights to privacy. Use "the untouchables" activity to open up communication on this topic. Have a free, open discussion of your feelings about personal possessions and come to some kind of consensus on a policy for personal possession rights.

9. *For families with young children:* Have a show-and-tell with your children. Each person, including parents, should bring his favorite personal possession and show it to the rest of the family. Because young children will probably bring toys, you might want to take a few minutes to play with them.

Tell the following story about Danny's broken plane. It will help your children understand the importance of respecting other people's personal belongings.

10. *Story of Danny's broken plane.* Danny is five years old and is in kindergarten. Danny's mother had a beautiful

43

glass figurine of a boy and his dog. Danny's mother always said, "You can look at it, Danny, but never pick it up. If you dropped it, it would break."

Danny wanted to pick it up just once. One day he decided, "I'll be very careful and just pick it up a little." Danny picked up the figurine. He dropped it, and it broke.

Danny's mother was very sad that her figurine was broken. "Danny," she said, "you disobeyed when you picked up my doll. Now it is broken and cannot be fixed."

Danny wished he had not touched it. But it was too late. It was already broken.

Later that day, Danny's friend Adam came over to play. "That's a pretty plane, Danny," Adam said. "Can I fly it?"

"No, it's only to look at," replied Danny. But when Danny left the room to get some cookies, Adam tried to fly the plane. And it broke. Danny cried because that was a special plane. His father had given it to him on his last birthday. Now it was ruined.

That evening Danny told his father what happened. "Danny," his father said, "I know you are very sad that the plane is broken. That's just how your mother feels about her broken figurine. People always feel sad when something special is broken."

"They sure do," Danny replied. "I'm going to leave other people's things alone from now on."

Discuss this story with your children.
—Why was Danny's mother sad?
—How did Danny feel when Adam broke his plane?
—How would you have felt?
—Can you think of a rule about touching other people's things? (Always ask before you touch.)

You might want to give your child a small present. Tell him that the present is his, and no one is to touch it unless they ask him first.

Family Time Three—
Caring for Family Possessions
Goal: During this family time each family member should come to understand the value of family possessions and feel his responsibility to help care for them.

For Parents: In most homes the care of family possessions is a continual problem. Parents end up maintaining most of them. Children need to be taught early in their lives that family possessions are the responsibility of the entire family.

The activities in this family time are designed to help you communicate this value to your children. Choose the activities that you feel your family will enjoy.

1. *Family possessions:* Start this family time by having members tell what their favorite family possession is and why (such things as car, television, dog, house, etc.).

Next give each member a pencil and piece of paper. Have him draw a stick-figure picture of the family at the top. Under the picture on the left side of the paper, have him list in a column all the family possessions he can think of in the next five minutes. To the right of each family possession have everyone list the person or persons who are responsible for taking care of that item.

Share your lists with one another and discuss the following:

—What is a family possession?
—How do you feel when your favorite family possession is misused?
—What responsibility does each family member have in the care of these possessions?
—What happens when someone does not care properly for a family possession?
—Which of our family possessions need better care? How could the family take better care of them?

2. *Possession problems.* Colossians 3:12-17 gives a list of qualities that Christians should posses. Read this Scripture passage aloud and have the family decide on two qualities that, if lived out, would help everyone to be more responsible with family possessions.

The following are four problems about family possessions that occur in many homes. Read each of these and discuss what the person or persons mentioned in the case studies would do differently if he were "living out" the two qualities from Colossians.

—Roger has a steady girl friend and likes to use the family car on dates. Many times Roger's father finds the gas tank empty when he gets ready to go to work in the morning. When it is time to clean the car on Saturday, Roger says he can't help because of his studies and part-time job.
—Cindy, age eight, likes to listen to the family records, but lately she has not been putting them away properly and several scratches have been noticed on them.
—Dishes are a big hassle at the Johnsons. Not only do the Johnson children complain bitterly about having to do the dishes, but they also usually just leave glasses and plates wherever they happen to be eating.
—The Rollins family has several family games they all enjoy playing. They each take turns putting the games away after they have been used. But Chris is usually careless and just "throws" the games into their boxes. The games are beginning to look terrible and the rest of the family is upset.

3. *Family possession project.* Decide on a family possession that needs some tender loving care. Use the rest of your family time working on that project. You might wash the car, clean the yard, wash the windows, clean up the camping equipment, etc.

4. *A personal commitment to care for family possessions.* Have each family member finish the following open-ended sentences:

"A family possession I sometimes misuse is _____ .

In the future I will be more responsible by _____

_____ ."

_____

Signed _____

5. *Money and possessions.* God expects the Christian family to use its money wisely. Proper care of family pos-

sessions is a good way to save money. Tell family members that because of the money the family will save as a result of their commitment to care for family possessions, you are going to treat them to something of their choice (within reason, of course).

6. *For families with teens.* In many homes the family car is a special problem. Discuss the following questions and adopt some type of mutually acceptable guideline for car use.

—What are the priorities for car use?
—Who is responsible for upkeep of the car? What things must be taken care of?
—Who pays for damage done to the car?
—What should the procedure be for asking for permission to use the car?
—What limitations should be imposed if the car is misused?

7. *For families with young children.* Even young children can learn that they are responsible to care for family possessions.

Prepare four sheets of paper. From magazines, cut pictures of a mother, father, children, and family. Paste one of these at the top of each piece of paper.

Next, cut out about fifteen pictures of various family and personal possessions. For instance, you might cut out pictures of a television set, house, car, doll, perfume, toy, stove, dog, game, etc.

Place the four papers and the fifteen pictures in front of your children on a table. Tell them to look at the pictures, decide to whom each item belongs, and then paste each picture on the right page. For example, the picture of the perfume might go on the paper with the picture of the mother, while the picture of the television would be pasted on the paper with the picture of the family at the top.

When this project is completed, discuss the pictures. Talk about the fact that some things are personal possessions and others are family possessions.

Ask why the car is a family possession. (Because the whole family uses it.) Talk about some ways that the whole family can keep the car clean. Ask what happens when family members leave papers, toys, and other items in the car. Use this procedure to discuss each of the pictures.

Choose a family possession that you can work on together, such as cleaning the car or the yard. Let your young children help you work on this project. As you work, discuss the importance of each family member helping to care for family possessions.

Praise your young children for their help. Have an extra special treat for the young workers.

Family Night Four—
Listening Is Fun

Goal: This family evening is designed to increase communication in the family as members sharpen their listening skills.

For Parents: It is estimated that we hear only about 25 percent of what is said. If that is so, then there must be something wrong with the way we listen!

Family communication is extremely important. Listening is a crucial part of communication.

As parents, we need to be examples of good listeners. Do we hear our children through, even when we disagree? Are we sensitive enough to look behind their words to what they really mean?

During this family night, your family should increase its sensitivity toward one another as they learn to listen in love.

Choose the activities that fit your needs and interests. Are you listening?

1. *Gossip.* Write on a slip of paper a sentence about any subject. Whisper the sentence into the ear of another family member. He whispers the same sentence, exactly as he hears it, into the ear of the person next to him, who in turn repeats it to the next person. After everyone has heard the sentence, the last person repeats it aloud. Compare what he says with the original sentence.

Was the sentence given by the last person different from the original? What does that teach about listening?

2. *Concentrate.* Tell family members that you are going to play a listening game that takes concentration. Have one person stand in the center of the room. He walks up to another family member, touches a part of his own body, and says, "This is my leg" (or foot, finger, head, etc.) as he points to a part *different* than the one he has named, such as an eye. The person he is standing before must point to whatever has been named (in the preceding case, the leg) and identify the part pointed to by the leader (saying, for example, "This is my eye") before the leader counts to 10.

If he fails the listening test before the count of 10 he replaces the one in the center.

3. *Listen, listen, listen.* Read Proverbs 18:13. What does this teach about listening? Have each person give an example of how this verse is true.

4. *Your third ear.* Do you have a third ear? If not, you can start growing one right now. Develop a sensitivity to what a person is really saying. A third ear hears beyond words and tries to understand underlying thoughts and feelings. Discuss:
 —How do you feel when you know someone is
   really not listening?
 —Do you sometimes feel a need for someone to
   listen to you in an understanding way?
 —How do you think someone else feels when
   he knows you are not really listening?
 —Name three ways you could be a better listener.

5. *The longest minute in the world.* Let each family member, in turn, talk for one minute. After a family member has completed his one-minute ordeal, the rest of the family should discuss what they think he said. Then he shares with the family what he meant to say. What were the differences? What does this say about listening? Let each family member have a turn.

6. *For families with teens:* Parents and teens can take the following test. After completing it, share the results. Discuss how listening in the home can be improved.

49

—Do you wait until (parent/teen) is through talking
    before having your say?
—Do you respect (parent/teen) opinions?
—When (parent/teen) talks, do you pretend you're
    listening when you're not?
—When (parent/teen) talks, do you let your preconceived
    ideas screen out what he is saying?
—When (parent/teen) talks do you listen or are you
    thinking about what you are going to say when he is
    finished?

7. *For families with young children:* Young children will
become good listeners if their parents set a good example
by listening attentively to what they and other people have
to say. Make sure that you give them a good example to
follow.

Another way to help young children become good listeners is to have them memorize short lines or stories. Read
the lines or stories to your child in short sections and have
him repeat it. He will soon have it memorized. Help your
child learn the following poem:

God gave me two ears and I can hear *(point to ear).*
    I can hear my daddy *(point to Father).*
    I can hear my mommy *(point to Mother).*
    I can hear my brothers and sisters *(point to
        brothers and sisters).*
    When they speak I listen *(cup hands around ears).*
    Thank You, God, for ears *(fold hands and look up).*

Discussion Questions

1. What is the strongest feeling you experience when you hear the words, "family togetherness"?

2. What kind of family togetherness did you experience in your family when you were growing up?

3. On a scale of one to ten, how would you rate family togetherness in your family right now?

4. What is the greatest obstacle in your family to doing things together?

5. Have you ever tried regular family times? What was the result?

6. The author gives four guidelines for successful family times. Which of these guidelines do you need to observe when having family times in your home?

7. Try one of the family times suggested in this chapter with your family.

8. What was the result of your family time? Did everyone have fun? Were there frustrations? What could you do differently to have a more successful family time?

9. Are regular family times for you? Why or why not?

10. What one thing will you do to develop more family togetherness in your home?

CHAPTER 4

Building Family Togetherness at the Dinner Hour

Marjorie Holmes, in *You and I and Yesterday*, laments the tragic loss of the dinner hour in American homes:

> Whatever happened to the family dinner hour? or "supper" as we called it in our small town? That time at the end of the day when everybody was summoned to wash up and sit down together to share a common meal. A time not only to eat but to talk to each other, even if you sometimes quarreled. A time and place where you could laugh, joke, exchange ideas, tell stories, dump your troubles. (Yes, and learn your manners.)
>   Surely its disappearance has a lot to do with the much-lamented disintegration of the American family.[1]

Does Mrs. Holmes have reason to be alarmed? Is the family meal losing importance in American homes?

Yes, according to a study cited in *Today's Child* magazine. Dr. Paul A. Fine, psychological consultant to several food companies, explored several myths about the American family's eating habits. One common myth he attacks is that the family eats together regularly:

> *The myth:* Americans eat breakfasts and dinners together as a family, drawing spiritual as well as nutritional sustenance from the shared ritual.
>   *The reality:* Fine's survey revealed that families tend to

sit down to dinner together no more than three times a week and often less frequently. The dining rite is generally completed within 20 minutes. Three out of four families do not breakfast together; many skip breakfast entirely.[2]

Now why all this fuss about the family eating together? Is it really that important to family life? I believe it is. What happens when the family eats together—especially at the dinner hour—is an extremely important part of building family unity and teaching Christian values. By conversation at the dinner hour, listening, sharing, and communicating ideas and dreams, the family circle is drawn tighter with love and understanding.

The importance of the family meal is awesome. Sharing a meal with others creates a closeness that is tangible. I believe that God in His great family plan saw meals to be a source not only of physical strength but also of spiritual and emotional strength. Meals are a focal point of many Scriptures. It is significant that Jesus chose the Passover meal as one of His last major activities with His disciples before He died. Jesus had a purpose in this. He wanted His disciples, and all future Christians, to continue to have intimate fellowship with Him and each other on a regular basis. It is through this shared meal that the family of God remember Jesus' death.

If the family can be weakened by the loss of togetherness at the table, then the opposite is also true. By using the great potential of eating together as a family, parents can build family strength and solidarity.

Corrie ten Boom found such strength around the oval table in her home while she was growing up.

Can a piece of furniture be important? The oval table in our dining room was the gathering place for hopes and dreams, the listening place for prayers and petititions, and the loving place for joy and laughter. . . .

Conversations around the dinner table were lively because we all had stories or experiences we wanted to share. I believe that the great enjoyment of a family eating together is having this time when each person can be heard.

Father had a special talent in directing our talks so that no one would feel left out. We loved to tell personal stories, but were taught to laugh at ourselves, not to make fun of others.[3]

Corrie has rich memories of the "oval table" because someone saw its great potential for family growth. Her father determined to make eating together a focal point of family life, and God rewarded his effort by giving his children great strength.

I know of another father who decided that time around the table should have high priority. Paul Hunter, a young pastor in a little country church in Oregon, told me, "My dad really used our times around the table effectively. He was a busy pastor but the breakfast and dinner hour were sacred. He allowed nothing to interfere. At this time, we shared the news of the day, talked about important things, argued, discussed, and read a portion of Scripture. This is my warmest memory of growing up."

An interesting sidelight to the Hunter story is that Paul moved to Oregon to be close to his father, who pastors a nearby church. Why? "Because," Paul told me, "I want to continue to learn from my father. He has so much to offer a young pastor like myself."

Paul claims that "Even now when we spend the holidays with my parents, we linger at the table relishing each moment we spend together."

How to Build Dinner Hour Togetherness

A little planning will help you make the most out of your dinner hour. Not that everything needs to be structured—you should leave plenty of room for things to "just happen." Some simple planning, however, can increase the quality of the time you spend together.

Why not discuss this chapter with your spouse? Are you happy with the way things are going? Are there some activities mentioned in this chapter you would like to try? Set some goals. Could you have a "dinner hour" once a week? Twice a week? Would you like to try reading together?

To help you plan good times for your dinner hour, Janet and I have compiled a list of activities our family enjoyed when our children were at home.

54

Word of the week. Each week have a family member research in a Bible dictionary and share the meaning of a Bible word such as exile, high priest, Emmanuel, Christian, atonement, apostle, gospel, fast, Crete, revelation, etc. The person should read a verse in which the word is used. You might want to have each person start a dictionary of his own by writing the word and its meaning in a notebook or on an index card.

Question Box. Decorate a container of some kind and call it your "Question Box." Have each person write three Bible-related questions they would like to discuss on slips of paper. Put these in the box. Draw and discuss one question periodically. Encourage family member to put new questions in the box continually.

"What's the meaning, Father?" (Deuteronomy 6:20) Are you ready for this one, Dad? Occasionally let your children ask you a question. Your children might ask, "What do you think is the most important verse in *the Bible?" If the question is difficult and will take some research, give them a "question check" and answer it the next day.*

Give Mom and Dad the word. This activity will probably be very popular with your children. Let them give you a word and then you respond with a story from your past based on that word. For example, if your child gives you the word "Christmas," you could tell about an especially exciting Christmas you remember from your childhood.

Share a thought from private devotions. About once a week I ask someone in our family to share a thought from his personal devotions. I find it best to make the request before the dinner hour so the person can have his devotions if he has not already done so.

What about your day? Say a family member's name and a time of day, such as "John—11:00 a.m." John then must respond with a detailed account of what he was doing at that time.

55

Ask and answer. Select a passage of Scripture to read. Tell family members that, after the Scripture has been read aloud, each person must be ready to ask and answer a question. Read the passage and have each person close his Bible. One family member starts this activity by asking the person on his left a question about the Scripture. That person answers and then asks the person on his left a question. Continue this procedure until each family member has asked and answered a question.

Place mat fun. A family can have many good times at the dinner table by working together on place mats. Use shelf, construction or even typing paper for place mats. Here are some activities you can use for place mat fun:

1. Have each person draw a picture of a Bible verse or story.

2. Select a "thought of the day" and have each person write it at the top of his place mat. Thoughts can be Bible topics such as salvation, Jesus, Holy Spirit, sin, Satan, grace, patience, humility, etc. Give family members five minutes to write down all their thoughts about that word. Discuss the word as family members share their thoughts.

3. Fold your place mats in fourths. Have each person draw a continuous Bible story using the four panels.

4. Scramble the letters of a Bible word. For example, sin scrambled might look like *nis.* Have family members exchange place mats and try to figure out the scrambled words. Discuss the various words.

5. Select one family member to draw a picture of a Scripture verse or Bible story while the rest of the family tries to guess what he is drawing.

6. Have family members make an acrostic out of a Bible word. To make an acrostic you lwrite a word vertically on your place mat and then think of words that start with each letter. New words should be associated with the acrostic word, as shown below with the word JESUS.

J—Joy
E—Everlasting
S—Supreme
U—Unity
S—Saves

Have family members share their acrostics. Discuss the various words that are selected.

Read and explain. Have a family member read and explain a Scripture passage.

Read and comment. Have a family member read a Scripture verse. Then go around the family circle with each person commenting on what he feels the verse means, on what he likes about it or on an experience he has had in apply that verse to life.

Sermon search. We have had many good times with this activity. Sermon search starts at church and is completed at home. The following seven activities are for your family to do during the sermon. Assign two of these on a Sunday morning. After lunch (or at some other appropriate time) have your family share their completed activities and discuss the message.
1. Illustrate the sermon.
2. What was the main point?
3. What part of the sermon did I like best?
4. The sermon made me feel _____ .
5. I didn't understand _____ .
6. As a Christian I should _____ .
7. Prepare a quiz. Have each person prepare two questions about the sermon. Collect the questions and take the test. Who listened closest to the sermon?

News item. Clip out interesting news items and talk about them at the dinner table. There are many types of news items. Some show the world's need for Christ. Others show how God's love is put into practice. Still others are just interesting happenings. You might want to have one of your children select what he feels is the "news item of the week" and talk about it at the dinner hour. Whenever possible, use news items as a springboard for discussing Scriptural principles.

Discuss debate. You can have some lively times with this activity. Select a discussion topic, such as:

—Are most Christians hypocrites?
—Should a Christian ever tell a lie?
—Does God always answer our prayers the way
  we want Him to?
—Is an occasional drink of alcohol okay?

Tell family members that you will start this discussion and sometime during the discussion you will stop them and choose two persons to take opposite views and debate the issue for two minutes.

After the debate continue the discussion.

Last letter add-a-word. One family member starts this activity by saying a Bible word such as "John." The person on his left must say another Bible word starting with the last letter of the word just given. For example, he might say "Noah," because Noah starts with N, the last letter of John. See how many times you can go around the family circle with each person adding a word.

Who am I? Have someone think of a Bible person and ask, "Who am I?" Other members of the family, in turn, ask questions that can be answered yes or no about his identity. The person who correctly identifies the Bible character is the winner and is next to ask, "Who am I?"

Read together. Select a Bible book and read a chapter or two. Continue reading each evening until the book is finished.

Card clues. About once a week hide a card clue under a family member's plate. No one is allowed to look under his plate until the meal is over and Mom and Dad gives the signal. The person who discovers the card clue must read it aloud and follow the instructions.

Write the following instructions on index cards or make up clues of your own:
—Tell a funny story.
—Play follow the leader. The family must copy you
  for the next five minutes.
—You may ask a favor of Dad.
—Check under your beds for a surprise.

—Say something nice about the person on your right.
—Quote or read your favorite Scripture verse.
—Lead a song.
—Ask Mother a Bible question.
—Select a family member to sing a solo.
—Surprise! We are going out for ice cream cones.
—Pantomime an Old Testament story.
—Pantomime a New Testament story.
—Play "Who am I?" (you are it)
—Tell the funniest thing that happened to you this week.
—Tell a joke.
—Lead a discussion on why Judas betrayed Christ.
—Lead a discussion on why one thief on the cross
    trusted Jesus and the other didn't.
—Have everyone think of a number between 1 and 15.
    The one who comes closest must do a chore for you.
—-Congratulations! You have just won the Helper Award.
    During the next week you must do one helpful thing
    for each family member.
—Tell when you feel closest to God.

Problem—solution. This activity encourages family members to help one another with their problems. One family member tells the person on his left a personal problem. He might say, for example, "I'm having trouble with math at school and the teacher doesn't seem to care." The person on the left then shares a possible solution to that problem, perhaps, "Why don't you ask your teacher for an appointment and then ask him how you can improve?"

Continue around the table until each person states a problem and helps another with a solution.

Change the subject. For this activity you will need a medium-sized ball. After dinner, seat the family in a circle on the floor. Explain to your family that you will start talking about an interesting subject and at any moment during your conversation you may roll the ball to another family member. That person must start talking about a new subject of his own. When he wishes, that person may roll the ball to another family member, who must start a new subject. Continue the game until everyone has participated.

Extended dinner hour. Extend dinner time by reading aloud as a family when you have finished eating. We did this for years and found it to be an excellent source of family unity. An excellent bibliography for read-aloud family books can be found in *Honey for a Child's Heart* by Gladys Hunt.

Ties That Bind Us

Suppertime ... that final meal when the day was almost over. The tradition of the family table. In letting it slip away from us I'm afraid we've lost something precious. We've cheated our children, stunted their social growth, gagged their articulation, cut off too early those ties that nature meant for us. The ties that bind us to people in the same family, people who represent comfort, security, nourishment, not only of body but of spirit. Ties that used to be gathered up at the close of a day and drawn together, if not always in peace, at least in fellowship and caring ...

I wish that by some magic I could step to the door and hear it echoing from every house for blocks. *"Suppertime! Come on in, supper's ready!"* [4]

Our family enthusiastically agrees! We feel that those "ties that bind us" can be strengthened through good times at the dinner hour.

------

[1] Marjorie Holmes, *You and I and Yesterday* (New York: Bantam Books, 1974), p. 148.

[2] "Family Eating Study Yields Food for Thought," *Today's Child*, vol. 22 (March 1974), p. 1.

[3] Corrie ten Boom, *In My Father's House.* Old Tappan, NJ: Fleming H. Revell Co., 1976, pp. 61, 62.

[4] Holmes, pp. 156, 157.

Discussion Questions

1. Use three words to describe your dinner hours.

2. Do you agree or disagree with the author's view that the times of eating together are an important part of building family togetherness and teaching Christian values?

3. How often does your family eat meals together? On a scale of one to ten, how effective are these times in building family togetherness and teaching Christian values?

4. What is your greatest frustration about mealtimes at your house?

5. What were mealtimes like when you were growing up? How have your early experiences affected your own family's mealtime rituals?

6. Try the "Give Mom and Dad the word" activity (page 55) this week at a mealtime. How did it work for you?

7. What are two possible ways mealtimes could be improved in your home?

8. What is the greatest obstacle you must overcome to make mealtimes more successful in your home?

9. What is your strongest feeling after reading this chapter?

10. What is one thing you can do to use mealtimes to build family togetherness in your home?

Section 2

Basics of Parenting

CHAPTER 5

Right On Schedule

Part 1: Birth to Five

Your Child's Actions

"What has happened to my baby?" you say as you look at your "grown up" little 18-month-old child. "It seems like just yesterday," you think, "that he was a helpless little thing that needed constant care. Now I'm the one that is helpless—trying to keep up with him!"

The last 18 months have gone incredibly fast. So many accomplishments have been packed into them. There was that glorious night at 16 weeks when he slept the whole night through. "Great kid," you thought. "He's going to be all right after all."

Then there was that first non-gas-aided smile. A real smile! "This child's way ahead of schedule," you and your spouse agreed.

Six months and look at what he can do now. He sits (with occasional roll-overs), he bounces; he shows signs, according to his father, of exceptional athletic potential.

A few more months have slipped by. Now, according to his grandparents and several other unbiased adults, the consensus is that your child is months ahead of schedule, a truly brilliant child. At ten months of age he is definitely saying some words. At least those close to him are quite sure. He is mastering the difficult skill of pat-a-cake. Occasional misses are overshadowed by the sheer brilliance of the hits. The real news, however, is that he is creeping. That's right, he now has his own motor. He's on the move. You have your own human vacuum cleaner, picking fuzz off the rug and eating it—and whatever else is in the way. Just what you've always wanted, a rug rat! Not only is he creeping, but you are starting to train him in the great feat of walking. It's going to happen soon, you're sure.

Flash by five months. What has happened is unbelievable. He not only walks but is a regular little locomotive. He climbs (and falls). Stairs are hardly a challenge. The word is out that the little guy gets into just about everything. You're sure that this is just temporary and will ease up in the next few weeks. He has this great game that he likes to play. It goes something like this—"I throw it down and you pick it up."

The time flies by. Your child is now 18 months old. He is unbelievable in several ways. This adorable child of yours has become a bundle of frustrations to you. It seems like the only word he knows anymore is "no." You ask him to come to you and he runs in the opposite direction. On a scale of 1—10 his rating in patience is minus 10. You had a heart-to-heart talk with your spouse last night. The topic of the discussion, "What are we doing wrong?"

Well, cheer up. Things will get better and things will get worse. Eighteen months is not one of the better ages, but it is not the worst age either. If it will make you feel any better, just remember that parents of most 18-month-old children go through the same thing. It is called "growing up," and like the other stages we will discuss, your child simply must pass through it.

Children struggle toward maturity; as parents, we must struggle with them. They go through delightful stages and they go through disastrous stages. Actually each stage of your child's life brings with it joys and frustrations. The important thing is to remember that someday you will launch a happy, successful child. Then you will breathe a deep sigh of relief and say, "It was worth it all."

What I have been describing is the "typical" behavior of

children at specific ages in their life. The problem with describing "typical" behavior is that there is no "typical" child. Your child may pass through a stage that I have described slower or faster than "typical." *Don't worry about that.* The characteristics of children at different ages do vary. The important thing to learn is that children go through similar stages in the growing up process. The intensity of what they experience (and what you experience) may be lower or higher than I describe. The value of knowing what to expect from your child at different ages is the security of knowing things are normal. Your child is not headed for a life of crime. *You are not an incompetent parent.* Your child is simply going through what all children go through on their rough road to maturity.

Please understand me at this point. I am not saying that because your child is going through an obnoxious stage and misbehaving terribly, you should sit idly by explaining to your terrorized neighbors, "It's simply his age. He'll grow out of it." Discipline is always in order. Stages or no stages, it is our primary goal to raise responsible children. Responsible children are a result of responsible training. Poor behavior calls for appropriate action. Let me share a warning. Not all behavior is a sole result of the stage. Children do not always "grow out" of irresponsible behavior. Sometimes a behavior can become ingrained. You must deal with chronic misbehavior in very specific ways.

A knowledge of developmental stages will help keep your perspective of your child a realistic one. Knowing what "typical" behavior is for a child at a given age can help your expectations and enable you to cope. Let's move on with our characteristics of ages.

Terrible twos. You have heard the expression, "terrible twos," and if you have already ushered a child through this stage, I need say no more. I have often referred to this stage as a "disease." The problem is that there are no pills you can give your child—or take yourself. You simply must tough it out.

Actually the first part of your child's second year starts out smoothly. You have coped with his 18-month-old tirades, and at 24 months you find he is much easier to live with. He is not as demanding. He has just a hint of patience. There are even occasions (shock of all shocks) when he tries to please others. You are beginning to think there is hope for your child after all.

Then it hits! Two and a half. The mere mention of this age is enough to put fear in the heart of the bravest of parents. I will never forget when Liesl, our middle daughter, hit this age. We called her the "leg whiner." She wrapped herself around her mother's leg and whined in the most irritating tone imaginable, "I want my mamma!" I was afraid Janet would have a permanent limp from dragging Liesl around the house.

Liesl was totally inflexible. Everything had to be done in an exact routine. When we put her to bed, we had to sit down on the bed first, ask her a Bible question second, kiss her on the forehead third, turn off the light fourth. There could be no changing of that sequence.

Liesl was also demanding. She wanted to run the house. "Me do," was her favorite expression. Add to this endless questions (the same one 29 times) and the demand to read a story for the 15th time and you have the seeds of parental insanity. I later found out that Liesl was a classic example of a "terrible two."

Terrific threes. Things get better where your child reaches three. Believe it or not, the word "yes" is back in your child's vocabulary. Sharing with others becomes a little easier. The rituals and demands have subsided. Your child seems secure and is starting to enjoy his relationship with others. Your three-year-old's vocabulary has increased, and that in itself makes him a rather delightful child. He can talk and you can reason with him.

Your delightful three-year-old, however, at about three-and-a-half, starts making some changes. These can be seen mostly in his relationships. He starts becoming insecure both in his relationship with you and with his friends. He might accuse you of not loving him or his friends of not liking him.

Frantic fours. Frantic may be too mild a word to describe the actions of a typical four-year-old. You have probably seen this kid in action. He kicks his friends, he pokes, he pushes, and he is loud and silly when he is not mad at someone.

The words he loves to use most are the ones that have to do with elimination. Talk about a nasty mouth, this kid's got it. This is the age when you start investigating your child's friends. You are quite sure he is being taught bad language by the unruly kids down the street. More correctly, children of this age are experiencing what they see as the sheer joy of trying to "out-nasty" one another.

Not only is the four-year-old crude and rough, he brags about it. In his eyes he is the toughest and greatest. Just ask him.

You have to be tough with a four-year-old. His behavior demands it. He has to have the limits set, because he is in no frame of mind to set those limits for himself.

The closer your four-year-old gets to five, the more reasonable he becomes. He starts using more self control. He is less of a bragger and tends to clean his language up. And why shouldn't he? After all, he is approaching the most delightful age of all.

Fabulous fives. You deserve this. It's about time someone did you a favor. Most people agree that five years of ages is about the most delightful age your child will go through. At this age you heave a huge sigh of relief and congratulate yourself on a job well done. All that work has paid off. Your child is now easy to get along with, secure, and reliable. Not only is your five-year-old angel well behaved, he thinks you're the greatest. That's a good combination in anyone's mind—a child that is well-behaved, a joy to be around, and one that thinks you can do no wrong. Wouldn't it be great if you could freeze your child at this age? Of course, if that was possible, you would miss some of the great times that are ahead of you.

Your Child's Thoughts
"I've got a big problem with my five-year-old daughter," says a distraught mother. "She simply refuses to share with her friends. There doesn't seem to be any way to get through to her."

This mother, like most of us, forgot that there is a huge difference between the way children and adults think. There is a reason why this mother's little girl has problems learning to share. Adults are able to think in concepts, and preschool children have a very limited use of this facility. A concept is an abstract idea generalized from particulars.

Let's use sharing as an example. As an adult you have a well-developed concept of sharing because you have gathered a lot of particulars over the years. You were taught, by your parents and other adults, that it was good to share with others. As you grew older, you experienced a good feeling when people shared with you. You also found out that you felt good when sharing something with another person. You came to realize that sharing is an expression of love, and that God wants you to express your love to others in this way. You came to sense when people around you had needs that you could help with. Your sharing moved from strictly physical things to sharing emotional support with others. You were able to "put yourself in another person's place," to feel his needs. All these experiences combined to form your concept of sharing. This took years. *When you were four* it is doubtful that you cared any more about sharing than your four-year-old does now. Not because you were selfish, but simply because in God's plan for young minds you had not experienced enough of life to think maturely.

Does this mean that we do not teach our child to share because he does not fully understand this concept? Obviously not. As we teach him about sharing, we are helping him develop a concept of sharing. Don't be surprised when your preschool child seems very selfish. Have confidence that what you are teaching him about sharing, which he seems to totally ignore, will some day pay off.

Forgiveness is another concept that we are anxious for our children to develop. I can remember talking to Heidi, our oldest daughter, about a school problem one day. A girl had done something thoughtless to hurt her. Heidi explained to me her plan of attack. She was going to write notes spreading all kinds of nasty rumors about this girl. I talked to Heidi about what Jesus would want her to do. I explained the quality of returning good for evil. Can you guess what her response was? After all my eloquent sermonizing she said, "But Dad, she hurt me and I have a right to hurt her."

Think again of all the experiences that have gone into building your concept of forgiveness. You understand God's forgiveness of you through Jesus Christ. You understand unconditional love. You know what it is to have the continual forgiveness of God even though you do not deserve it. You understand grace. You have had experiences where you have found great joy in your life from forgiving someone who has wronged you. You know from Scripture that forgiveness is a gift, and that as a Christian you sometimes give the gift of forgiveness to someone who does not deserve it. But in spite of our experiences, we as adults struggle with few concepts more than the concept of forgiveness. Is it any surprise that a young child has a tremendous struggle understanding the meaning of returning good for evil?

Other areas strike dread to the heart of a parent. You catch your child in a lie. This happens several times. Your way of thinking dominates. "My child is a liar," you think. Your child, however, has no concept of what a liar is. He simply has found it more expedient to tell a lie than to get into trouble. It makes sense to him. Over a period of time we teach our child that lying is wrong, and there are consequences to his actions. He slowly learns the concept of truthfulness.

Your child takes something that is not his. He does this several times. That dread comes back. "I am raising a thief," you think. Your child, however, has no concept of what it is to be a thief. He saw something he wanted and in his self-centered world took it, with hardly a thought to the consequences. You teach your child to be honest, but at the same time recognizing that at four, five, six, and seven there will still be some instances of him taking things that are not his and then lying about it.

It is important to remember that children have inaccurate concepts because they simply do not have enough information about a particular subject. They have just not lived long enough yet. The following dialogue illustrates a child's inaccuracy in concepts in a humorous way.

Our son, Rusty, six, was showing off a new toy racing car to a seven-year-old friend.

"This car," he boasted, "goes faster than infinity miles an hour."

"Infinity isn't fast," said his friend.

"It is, too," protested Rusty. "It's the fastest you can go— and this car goes one hundred miles an hour faster."

"Infinity is not either a fastness," said his friend. "It's a place you go in the Army, like a hospital, when you get hurt." Rusty was both convinced and undaunted.

"All right, then," he fumed. "I'll go to your infinity after I get crashed up going faster than infinity miles an hour in this car."[1]

Just as there is order to physical growth, there is order to mental growth and concept development in your child. The great Swiss psychologist, Jean Piaget, has developed a highly acclaimed theory of mental development in children. He suggests that a child will go through four periods on the way to mature reasoning.

Sensorimotor Period (birth to approximately two). Think of your 10-month-old for a moment, crawling on the rug—picking up fuzz and methodically devouring every eatable sized object in his way. He is exploring his environment in the only way he knows—through sensorimotor channels. Or think of your two-year-old for a moment. You visit a friend who does not have small children. You leave her house with a migraine headache from the tension of wondering what your child will reach for next. Again, he is exploring his environment in the way God designed for him at this age. You visit another friend who also has a young baby. Your baby sticks his finger in your friend's baby's eye. He is simply exploring his environment through sensorimotor channels.

This same process continues, to some degree, through his preschool and elementary school years. Follow any child into a store and watch how hard it is for him not to touch, or taste, or smell everything in sight. His learning is through the senses—sight, smell, feeling, and hearing.

Preoperational Thought (approximately 2—7). During this period of a child's life, he is not able to use certain

72

mental operations that are needed for mature reasoning. He can classify, but not more than one property at a time. For example, he can understand that he lives in Napa, but it is impossible for him to understand how he can live in Napa and in California at the same time.

If you had two short glasses of water and poured one glass into a taller, thinner glass, the child of this age would have great difficulty realizing that the amount of water in the containers remained the same. This is because he sees things in terms of how they look rather than on a basis of mental operations.

Concrete Operations (7—11 or 12). During the ages of 7—11 your child will progressively grow in his ability to use mental operations by which he can come to logical conclusions. He will be able to make multiple classifications, such as: Napa is in California, California is in the United States, and the United States is in the world. He can compare, contrast, find other examples, predict some consequences, and apply rules to various situations. During this time he is better able to deal with concrete data than with abstract ideas.

Formal Operations (11 or 12 and up). At about eleven or twelve the child enters the level of formal operations. He is now able to think in abstract terms. His ability to think on abstracts grows steadily until as a young adult the ability to think in concepts is well-developed. He is now able to deal with the concepts of sin, forgiveness, and truthfulness on a mature level. He is able to mentally put himself in another's place to get a sense of how they feel. He is able to deal with God as the Father, the Son, and the Holy Spirit. He is able to see consequences or results.

God, in His infinite wisdom, created a logical sequence in our physical and mental growth. We can't hurry our child's mental growth any more than we can hurry his physical growth. He must go through certain stages of reasoning. Knowing how our children think can help us both accept our children and deal with their inappropriate behavior in a reasonable manner.

Steps in Developmental Tasks

So far we have described the stages in behavior your child will go through at the first five years of his life and the development of his thinking processes. Now we are going to look at some developmental tasks that your child must achieve if he is going to be a happy, well-adjusted adult. "A developmental task is a task which arises at, or about, a certain period in the life of the individual, successful achievement of which leads to his happiness and to success with later tasks, while failure leads to unhappiness in the individual, disapproval by society, and difficulty in later tasks."[3]

According to Erik Erikson, your child must go through three of these tasks during his preschool years and two more from ages six to eleven. They are as follows:

(1) Sense of Trust (one year)
(2) Sense of Autonomy (toddler—two years)
(3) Sense of Initiative (three—five years)
(4) Sense of Industry and Accomplishment (six—eleven years)
(5) Sense of Ego Identity (early adolescence)
(6) Sense of Intimacy (later adolescence)

Your child learned a *sense of trust* from you during his first months. As loving mothers and fathers, you met your child's physical and emotional needs of love and belonging. Because he had his basic needs met by you, your child developed a sense of trust.

Almost before you were ready for it, your sweet little toddler started his obnoxious pilgrimage toward a *sense of autonomy.* You remember it well. His favorite expression was "Me do" as he marched defiantly toward independence. He was starting to answer the questions, "Who am I?" and "What can I do?" Your child was struggling to see himself as separate from you.

Based on satisfying experiences of trust and autonomy, your three-year-old child was ready to begin the third stage of a *sense of initiative.* With a greatly expanded world before him, your child started to initiate social relationships, expand family relationships, and develop a conscience.

Part Two: First—Sixth Grade

Now your school-age child is ready for the fourth state, a *sense of industry and accomplishment*. He is ready for a larger world of thought and action. Your child is now starting to experience the satisfaction of developing skills and demonstrating his abilities.

With the successful completion of the fourth stage, your child will enter the difficult fifth stage of a *sense of ego identity*. During this time of early adolescence, your young person will seek to clarify his role in society in terms of who he is and what he will become.

With a solid sense of who he is, your teenager will be ready to tackle the sixth stage of a *sense of intimacy*. A sense of intimacy, or the capacity to be intimate, is necessary for establishing heterosexual relationships. A solid marriage is possible only when a person has successfully worked through this stage.

Development Tasks of the School-Age Child

For your child to achieve a *sense of industry and accomplishment*, he must accomplish certain developmental tasks. Robert J. Havighurst lists nine tasks a school-age child must learn in order to be a happy, productive, and successful person. These nine tasks are grouped under three great pushes that affect a child's development. They are:

1. The social push, thrusting the child out of the home and into the peer group.
2. The physical push into the world of games and work requiring neuromuscular skills.
3. The intellectual push into the world of adult concepts, logic, symbolism, communication, and psychological environment and structure.[4]

Jesus was faced with these three same pushes when he was growing up in Nazareth. "And Jesus kept increasing in wisdom and stature, and in favor with God and men" (Luke 2:52).

Jesus was human as well as divine, and thus was subject to some of the same laws of human development that other children encountered. Jesus experienced the *intellectual push* as He grew in wisdom, the *physical push* as He grew in stature, and the *social push* as He grew in favor with men. There is a fourth push that secular writers do not deal with, that is the *spiritual push* as Jesus increased in favor with God.

We will now look at the nine specific developmental tasks that your child must accomplish during his school age years.

1. Learning physical skills necessary for ordinary games. The school-age years are a time when the general growth of muscle, bone, and coordination paves the way for your child to develop important skills. He learns to ride a bike, swim, throw a ball, climb trees, handle simple tools, and play physically strenuous games. These physical skills are important to your child. The peer group rewards a child for success in the area of physical skills; a child who lacks skills will sometimes be rejected by the peer group. Children feel good about themselves when they start to master their bodies and develop skills. As parents we need to understand the importance of this task. We can provide opportunities for our children to learn to play softball, swim, use tools, etc. Some children love physical activity, have a high degree of natural coordination and do not need much encouragement. Other children need to be encouraged to develop their physical skills. We need to work with them to develop this important part of their life.

2. Building wholesome attitudes toward oneself as a growing organism. It is important to help your child develop wholesome attitudes about himself as a growing organism. This is a vital attitude that God wants all of us to develop. "I urge you therefore, brethren, by the mercies of God, to present your bodies a living and holy sacrifice, acceptable to God, which is your spiritual service of worship" (Romans 12:1).

We must help our children develop habits of cleanliness. Children are judged by their physical appearance, both by peers and adults. There needs to be a balance here. We should never encourage the thinking that outer beauty is more important than inner beauty.

Healthy habits of exercise, diet, and sleep should be encouraged at an early age. As Americans, we have notoriously bad eating habits; many are overweight, which causes physical as well as psychological problems. Junk food is provided in abundance in many homes. We need to take a hard look at the eating habits our children are developing. Too much refined sugar can have detrimental effects on the mental and physical health of your children.

We need to help our children develop a wholesome attitude about their sexuality. Two things are important here: the parents wholesome attitude about their own sexuality, and their willingness to talk openly with their children.

3. *Learning to get along with age-mates.* One of the most important tasks your child has to learn is how to get along with age-mates. The school-age years provide the perfect opportunity. How well your child learns to socialize will determine to a large extent his success in life. Seldom does intelligence or physical skills compensate for a lack of skill in personal relationships.

Walk around any schoolyard and you will find little clumps of girls and boys, whispering, chasing, and playing games. What looks to be random groupings are not random at all. These children have competed to become part of the group. Within these groups children learn to relate to one another. They learn tolerance, teamwork, and loyalty; they also learn the pain of rejection. Some of the greatest lessons of life are learned within these groups. Your child learns that there are other lifestyles and other attitudes. It seems that enemies are just as important as friends during this time. Those outside the group are really outsiders.

By the way, these groups are sex-segregated. Heaven forbid if a girl should ever penetrate a boy's group or a boy a girl's group. The closest contact that most boys and girls have during elementary school is through "chasing," the favorite sport of all. There does seem to be more boy-girl activity with children reaching puberty so quickly.

With this give-and-take of the social group, your child begins to develop the skills in personal relationships he will need through life. As a parent, you are in a position to monitor those relationships and give good counsel. He has already watched how you handle personal relationships. Now he looks to you to refine his own skills with people. You are his teachers and the goal of your instruction is "love from a pure heart and a good conscience and a sincere faith" (1 Timothy 1:5).

If you see that your child has severe, chronic problems getting along with his age-mates and teachers, it is a signal that something is wrong. I would suggest seeing a professional counselor to gain insights into what is happening.

4. *Learning an appropriate masculine and feminine social role.* Appropriate masculine and feminine roles should be learned primarily within the family and be based upon Biblical precepts. What society teaches about masculine and feminine roles are man-made concepts and always reflect the *current* thinking of society. God's precepts are eternal, but there are differences in how these precepts are interpreted.

God has created differences in the sexes. "And God created man in His own image, in the image of God He created him; male and female He created them" (Genesis 1:27). Men and women are brought together to form a wonderful completeness in marriage. Scripture portrays man as the leader but not a director or as superior to women. That leadership is to be manifested in servanthood (Ephesians 5:21-33).

I believe it is possible to have much flexibility in husband/wife roles and still be true to Biblical precepts. Each husband and wife must work out the kind of masculine and feminine social roles they will model for their children.

5. *Developing fundamental skills in reading, writing, and calculating.* Reading, writing, and calculating are important in our highly technological world. To compete in the job market today, a person must have adequate skills in these basics. During the school-age years, the nervous system develops to the point where your child is capable of learning the skills of reading, writing, and calculating. These skills improve with special training and constant use.

6. *Developing concepts necessary for everyday living.* When your child enters school, he is limited to the use of several hundred basic concepts. By the time your child enters seventh grade, the concepts he is able to use will have grown to several thousand.

As parents you are very influential in your child's conceptual development. Some concepts children develop on their own. We help them develop other concepts by our input to them and how we observe the world.

7. *Developing conscience, morality, and a scale of values.* During the school-age years, you will have the tremendous responsibility of helping your child develop a Christian conscience, morality, and scale of values. Your values will become his values during these formative years. He will learn by example, by watching you live out Biblical values in your life. He will see what is really important to you by your attitudes and the way you use your time and resources (read Romans 12:2; 2 Timothy 3:16, 17). You are the most important influence in your childs life during these school-age years.

8. *Achieving personal independence.* Achieving independence means learning to make plans, following them through, and being able to act independently from parents and adults to a reasonable degree. With this independence, of course, we always encourage a dependence upon God (Proverbs 3:5, 6).

You are working yourself out of a job. In a few years your child will be out in the world on his own. It is crucial that you slowly but surely allow him more and more independence until he is able to stand on his own. He is already starting to realize that he will not be able to live at home all of his life. As he achieves the developmental tasks, he begins to see that someday he can make it on his own. Home, school, and peer group are all important laboratories in which your child's independence is cultivated.

9. *Developing attitudes toward social groups and institutions.* During these school-age years, your child will be developing feelings about religious, social, political, and ec-

onomic groups. Social attitudes are developed largely within the family. The school and peer groups are the other major contributing factors on how your child feels about social groups. You have the potential to help your child develop a healthy attitude toward the world he lives in.

Puberty

The declining age of puberty in our country is an additional factor some parents must face during the school-age years. One of our daughters reached puberty, that period when a person is first capable of reproducing sexually, two days after her eleventh birthday. "In the United States— where children mature up to a year earlier than in European countries—the average age at first menstruation has declined from 14.2 in 1900 to about 12.45 today."[5]

I suggest reading James Dobson's book, *Preparing for Adolescence*. This book, and his tapes on the same subject, can help you deal with this important area of your child's life.

Conclusion

Your child has a lot of hard work in front of him for the next few years. You will be able to help him complete the tasks that God and society have placed in front of him. Always remember that, other than God, you are the greatest influence in his life. Teachers or the peer group will never replace you as the major force in your child's life, if you maintain a responsible loving relationship with him.

---

[1]Marjorie Stith, *Understanding Children*. Nashville, TN: Convention Press, 1969, p. 71.

[2]Stith,pp. 64-66

[3]Anne Hitchcock Gilliland, *Understanding Preschoolers*. Nashville, TN: Convention Press, 1969, p. 55.

[4]Joyce Williams & Marjorie Stith, *Middle Childhood Behavior and Development*. New York: Macmillian Publishing Co., 1980, p. 35.

[5]Robert J. Havighurst, *Developmental Tasks and Education*. New York, David McKay Company, Inc., pp. 19-35.

Discussion Questions

1. Of the various ages mentioned in this chapter, which one have you enjoyed most? Which has been the most difficult for you to cope with?

2. Describe your preschool child. Would you call him delightful or disastrous? What are his current characteristics?

3. Has your child's lack of conceptual ability caused you anxiety? Explain.

4. How can expecting too much too soon in the area of forgiveness, honesty, and truthfulness cause undue stress on your and your child?

5. How can knowing the four areas of reasoning according to Piaget make your parenting task a little easier?

6. Do you agree or disagree with the author's view on what are appropriate masculine-feminine sex roles? How would you like your child to view his sex role?

7. Write down at least one example of your child's limited concept development. How does his concept development affect this behavior?

8. What indications do you see that your child is developing a Christian conscience and Biblical set of values?

9. How is your child going about his quest for independence and how is it affecting you?

10. After reading this chapter and evaluating myself, one thing I will change to improve my parenting is ...

CHAPTER 6

Who's in Charge?

What comes into your mind when you hear the word "discipline?" Sometimes the mention of this word will take us back to our childhood, to some unpleasant memories that we have of discipline in our own family. Perhaps the word "discipline" reminds us of some weaknesses or insecurities that we have in disciplining our own children.

Our attitude towards discipline, however, should be positive. *Discipline* and *disciple* come from the same root word.

> Anyone can punish a child, but only those who can make disciples of the children can truly discipline them. When we see discipline as a positive directive in life, we no longer do something to a child, but we do something for him or with him so that he will want to change for the better. The transfer from the outward must, so necessary in infancy, to the inward ought as the child grows in understanding, then becomes possible. Each occasion for constructive discipline is only another lesson in a lifelong process of learning, under the guidance of parents and God.[1]

Punishment is something we do *to* our children. Punishment focuses on the past. Discipline, on the other hand, is something we do *with* our children, focusing on the future. God's Word, speaking of discipline, says, "Yet to those who have been trained by it, afterwards it yields the peaceful fruit of righteousness" (Hebrews 12:11). All our attitudes and methods of discipline should focus on training our children for right living.

Stages of Morality

The goal of our discipline should be an "inner takeover" by our children. We are training them to someday discipline themselves. From the very first year of your child's birth, you are in a process of working yourself out of a job. Your main task as a parent is to help your children develop a mature Christian conscience. Conscience is that part of our personality that evaluates behavior. Conscience is the inner standard by which we live. But how does a mature Christian conscience develop? Bruce Narramore gives five stages in the development of our children's conscience. He calls these the five stages of morality.

Stage 1: Morality of physical restraint. During the early months, we simply have to restrain our children from dangers. They show almost no signs of conscience.

Stage 2: Fear and respect. The first signs of a conscience begin to appear at the end of the first year and during the second. Your child reaches out to grab a vase off the shelf, and you say, "No!" emphasized by a swat on his hand. He begins his lesson in fear and respect.

Stage 3: Internalized parent. During this time, children both consciously and unconsciously want to be like their mother and father. This process is known as identification or internalization. They gradually take on our attitudes and values.

Stage 4: Adolescent conscience. During this stage, the adolescent begins to reevaluate his standards. He begins to think for himself and no longer takes his parent's attitudes and values as law. The teenager rethinks his morality and comes to his own set of values.

Stage 5: Mature conscience. We should be able to see clear signs of the mature conscience by late adolescence and early adulthood. This means that the conscience should be free from many of the necessary controls of childhood and adolescence. A person with a mature conscience is motivated to Christian behavior because of his love of God and fellow man, not because of external controls and restraints.[2]

To move our children through Stage 1 to Stage 5, we must deal with their misbehavior. The methods of discipline we choose are crucial. However, to choose the best method of discipline, we must first try to determine why our child is misbehaving. There are many reasons for misbehavior. First of all, a child is basically self-centered. Some of his misbehavior is simply because he wants everything his own way. There are other times that a child misbehaves because he is sick or tired. Your child also may be trying to accomplish something by his misbehavior. I call this "Strategies of Misbehavior."

Strategies of Misbehavior

God has placed some significant needs in every human being. We all need to be loved, to be accepted for who we are, and to be successful. When these needs are not met in our lives, we become frustrated individuals. This affects our behavior. Since these needs are so overpowering, we strive to be loved and accepted. The problem comes when we use self-defeating strategies of behavior to accomplish our goals. A classic example is the person who has never really felt that he is accepted for who he is. As he moves into adulthood, he is totally absorbed in his work. He spends eighteen hours a day climbing up the corporate ladder. He achieves, but at the terrible price of his health and his family relationships. He still doesn't feel accepted and must move higher and higher. Every day he feels he must prove himself acceptable once again. This person's strategy for reaching the goal of acceptance is self-defeating. It will never work.

Children sometimes have strategies to meet the goals of feeling loved, accepted, and successful. Let's look at each strategy.

Strategy 1—"I'll Show Off"

Many times children will try to get attention in positive ways. When these ways do not achieve the desired results, children will use negative ways to be noticed. A child who continually shows off usually feels neglected, put down, and generally not accepted. He feels that getting attention through negative methods is better than getting no attention at all. A child with this strategy would rather be yelled at or punished than not noticed at all. When parents or teachers react to this misbehavior, the child feels that his strategy is working. Every stern look, angry response, or punishment assures that the child will use this strategy again.

There seems to be only two ways to help a child who is using this strategy to achieve his goal of being loved and accepted. The first is to ignore the behavior. I realize that this is extremely difficult to do when you are annoyed. The second way *must* accompany the first. Since the child is not feeling accepted, we must make a real effort to meet that need in our child's life. We need to praise his accomplishments. We need to focus on his uniqueness. We must focus on his positive behavior. We must learn that through changing his strategy from negative to positive behavior, he can achieve his goal of acceptance.

Strategy 2—"I'll Win"

Children use the "I'll Win" strategy more than any of the others. Almost all children involve their parents in power struggles. The goal that children have here is success, the need to feel confident and achieve. I'm sure that by now your child has involved you in many power struggles. Maybe you didn't realize they were power struggles, but chances are they were. Your child also probably won the power struggle. "How can that be?" you ask. "He is only four feet tall and I'm six feet tall and weigh 200 pounds. It doesn't seem fair that a little fellow can win a power struggle with a grown man, does it?" But that is what happens.

Anytime your child involves you in a power struggle you automatically lose. You might think you have won because he eventually obeys you, but believe me, *he has won.*

Let's see why. You walk into your child's room. "This room is a mess!" you shout. "Pick it up right now!"

"I'm busy," your child replies. "I'll pick it up in just a minute."

"I want it picked up right now!" you shout.

You come back an hour later and the room is only half picked up. This time you are furious. The battle goes on until the room is almost clean. You are exhausted but your child seems unscathed. In fact, he seems ready for another battle because thirty minutes later his room is a mess again.

It is natural for us to want to fight power with power. The only problem is that it doesn't work. Who wins in the power struggle over food at the table? Who wins when your child involves you in a power struggle over his painfully slow habits of putting his clothes on Sunday mornings? We must remember that any time a child involves us in a power struggle, he has won control. He has manipulated us into losing our cool. He has won.[1]

Power struggles are a strategy that our children use to meet their need for success, independence, and recognition. When these needs are blocked, they engage us in a power struggle. Affirming your child is one of the best ways of helping him meet his goal in a more constructive way. Give him as much room as possible to be independent and then praise his efforts. This does not mean we are giving up our authority as parents. We are always the authority in our child's life. He needs our rules. He needs our discipline. There are other ways, however, to handle potential power struggle situations. We will examine some of these a little later in this chapter as we look at methods of discipline.

Strategy 3—"I'll Get Revenge"

Your seven-year-old child has been picking on his five-year-old sister. You are embarrassed because you have been trying to hold a conversation with a friend. After several warnings, you tell you seven-year-old to go to his room. He screams at you, "You don't like me!" and wails down the hall. You apologize to your friend for this "unusual" disturbance and continue your conversation. You hear a loud banging on the wall. You go to your child's room and catch him pounding on the wall with his shoe. By this time you are infuriated, and you warn him that if he doesn't be quiet you are going to spank him as soon as the company leaves. You go back to your friend and try to ignore the various sounds coming from your child's room.

Your child has just engaged you in three strategies. First he tried the strategy of "I'll show off." Next he engaged you in a power struggle. Finally he decided to use his ultimate weapon, "revenge." A child who uses the strategy of revenge usually feels that he is not loved and accepted. Remember that these can be short-term emotions and not an accurate reflection of a child's overall feelings about himself. He feels that he has been hurt and is going to get revenge by striking back. This child has feelings of anger that he has not learned how to handle appropriately. It is a temptation for the parent to use a little revenge in return. This, of course, does not help the parent or the child. Remember that the child is striking out because he doesn't feel loved, accepted or successful. Those are painful feelings for anyone to have. This child needs love, praise, and *loving discipline.*

Strategy 4—"I'll Fail"

To me, this is the saddest strategy of all. It is pathetic when a child feels so inadequate that he will not even try for fear of failing once again. A child who uses this strategy is saying, "If I try, you will see how stupid I am. Therefore, I will not try." This child needs a tremendous amount of encouragement. Criticism only sends this child deeper into despair. This child needs to be encouraged for even the smallest achievement. This child needs to know that he is accepted no matter what his accomplishments. This child needs parents who will cherish his positive attributes. This child needs to know that God unconditionally loves and accepts him apart from any achievements he might make.

Methods of Discipline

It is important for a parent to know what strategies a child might be using and to know how to deal with these strategies. It is equally as important to know what methods of discipline to use when a child misbehaves. The following are methods of discipline, you may choose from when your child needs correction.

1. Communication

It may seem strange to list communication as a method of discipline, but remember the purpose of discipline is to train our child's conscience. This takes communication. We must always talk to our children about the positive consequences of good behavior and the negative consequences of poor behavior. What you really want for your child is a heart change, not merely a temporary change of behavior. Although I list communication as a separate method of discipline, it is also an integral part of all methods of discipline.

2. Negative Reinforcement (Time Out)

"Time Out," according to psychologist Jeff Bisaga, is the most effective method of discipline for young children. This works best with children who are nine and under. Here is how it works.

Your five-year-old child has been fighting with his sister. You've warned him once but he ignores you. You say to him, "Okay, Joey, you are disobeying so it looks like we need 'Time Out.'" Joey knows what "Time Out" is because this is a favorite method of discipline of his mother and father.

Joey is told to go to a specific corner of the house and stand, facing the wall, for two to five minutes, depending on the severity of the offense. This is a *borning corner.* It is not in Joey's room. It is in the most uninteresting place in the house. As Joey goes to the corner, he realizes that the five minutes does not start until he has stopped crying, protesting, or making other types of rebellious sounds. When the five minutes are over, Joey's mother says "time in" and has a chat with him about his behavior.

Here are some points to remember about "Time Out." For this method of discipline to be effective, it must be frequent and immediate. Your child needs to know that when he misbehaves he can expect "Time Out." If you reserve "Time Out" until after you have warned your child several times and are extremely frustrated, then you will not find this method of discipline effective. Another principle to remember is to not pile on additional minutes. The reason this discipline is effective with your children is that it is short enough for them to handle but long enough to cause discomfort. Don't start counting until your child is quietly standing in the corner. Set the buzzer on your stove so you don't have to keep checking the clock. It is very important to communicate with your child at the end of "Time Out." This will help him see the disadvantages of his actions and focus on correct behavior.

You can use "Time Out" for any type of childish irresponsibility. Outright defiance needs physical discipline which we will look at later.

3. Positive Reinforcement

Positive reinforcement means rewarding good behavior. This is an excellent method of discipline that we should use consistently with our children. A little praise, a hug, or a special privilege or reward for good behavior will remind our children that the consequences of good behavior are beneficial. This method of discipline works especially well with children who are trying to meet the goals of love, acceptance, and success through inappropriate strategies.

4. Extinction

When you recognize that your child is involved in trying to meet his goals of love, acceptance and success through "I'll Show Off," "I'll Win," "I'll Get Revenge," and "I'll Fail" strategies, extinction is a must. You must remove the reward he is receiving by his strategy of misbehavior. For example, if his strategy is "I'll Show Off," (attention) you must weaken this negative behavior by not responding in a negative or positive way to his showing off. This is extremely hard for most parents to do. We have a daughter that uses this strategy. I have to grit my teeth and use every ounce of self-discipline to not respond and reward her for her misbehavior. Over the years I have rewarded her far too often and in all cases, the behavior has gotten worse. When I have disciplined myself to ignore her attention-getting actions and focus on positive reinforcement, behavior has improved.

A classic example of this principle is the young child throwing a temper tantrum on the floor. He kicks and screams. If the parent either tries to console the child or discipline him in any way other than extinction, the child's plan has succeeded. You can be sure he will try it again.

5. Natural Consequences

God has built some natural discipline into His universe. Galatians 6:7 says, "Do not be deceived, God is not mocked; for whatever a man sows, this he will also reap."

Sometimes we need to let nature take its course if it does not mean extreme danger to our child. For example, your child is an avid bike rider. The problem is that he envisions himself as a miniature Evel Knievel (a daredevil motorcycle rider). You have warned him many times that he is going to either get hurt or damage his bike if he continues to ride carelessly over the speed ramp he and his friends have built. Your warnings and discipline have had little effect. You allow nature to discipline your child with the inevitable crash. Don't allow that bike to be fixed for awhile. Allow the cuts and bruises to teach a valuable lesson.

Eating is another area where natural consequences is sometimes the best method of discipline. Your child refuses to eat. You get into a power struggle with him at almost every meal. It is exhausting you and turning family meals into disaster. Since your child is involving you in a power struggle that you cannot win, natural consequences is the best method of discipline. Let nature take its course. Put the food on your child's plate and let him make a choice whether he eats it or not. There must be a hard and fast rule, however, that there can be no more food until the next meal—no dessert, no snacks, nothing. With the power struggle out of the way, nature will quickly take over. When your child gets hungry enough, he will eat. He is not going to starve!

6. Logical Consequences

Logical consequences differ from natural consequences because with logical consequences, we are involved in structuring the consequences of misbehavior. When our child misbehaves, we find a consequence that is closely associated with the action. The good thing about logical consequences is that it holds the child, not the parent, responsible for his decision. It takes parents out of the power struggle. Children learn from the consequences of their poor decisions.

Let's look at some examples of logical consequences:

"Can I go out and play now?" your child asks.

"No," you answer, "I explained to you this morning that if you wanted to play with Jimmy, that your chores would have to be done. I see that your room is not picked up and the wastepaper baskets have not been emptied."

"Oh, Mom," your child replies, "I'll do it later. Jimmy can only play for an hour."

"I'm sorry, Son, but you know the rule. When you are finished with your jobs, you may play with Jimmy."

In this situation, you have stayed out of a power struggle with your child. It was his choice not to do his chores and you have simply reminded him. If he wants to play, it is his responsibility to follow the rules. If your child had continued to press the matter, you would have refused to enter the power struggle and left the room.

Here is another example. You are trying to watch a TV program and your child seems intent on aggravating you by performing a show on the side. You give your child a choice. "Jamie, you may watch the TV show or go to your room. You decide which you would rather do." If your child continues to disturb you, then explain that she has chosen to go to her room.

7. Spanking

In recent years, it has been popular to picture spanking as barbarous. Some people have even gone so far as to say that it teaches children to strike back at others. I feel these philosophies are wrong. If spanking were wrong, then God would not have instructed us to use this method of discipline. Proverbs 13:24 says, "He who spares his rod hates his son, but he who loves him disciplines him diligently."

Spanking, however, should be reserved for situations of willful defiance or when other methods of discipline do not work. If there are other methods of discipline open to us then we should use them. We should always ask ourselves the question, "Which method of discipline will help my child develop self-discipline?" As a general rule, "Time Out," communication, and natural and logical consequences are much more effective methods of discipline than spanking because they train the child to make responsible choices.

With our first two children, I spanked too much. Because I was not in control of my own anger, spanking was often done to vent my frustrations. I did not think through the methods of discipline and choose the appropriate one. I was controlled by my emotions and went for the wooden spoon.

We should use spanking selectively and keep the following principles in mind:

—Never spank when you are not in control of your anger. Spanking is much more effective if done with a calm spirit. I know that sometimes we will violate this principle, but commit yourself to this ideal.

—Always explain to your child why you are spanking him, or ask him why he is being spanked. Tell him that he is loved but his behavior is unacceptable.

—Always use a neutral object, not your hand. Children have been seriously hurt by parents who use their hands to spank. A wooden spoon or ruler is adequate.

—Make sure your child feels pain but do not abuse him.

—After the spanking is over, give your child some kind of physical affection and say, "I love you."

Spanking, as a method of discipline, should be phased out by the time your child is in junior high.

Wear Your C.A.P.

I would like to give you one last idea for positive discipline in your home. When we start wondering who's in charge, it is time to put on our C.A.P.

C.A.P. is an acronym for

Communication,
Action, and
Persistence

Here is how putting on your C.A.P. works. Often when we feel that our children are in control it is because we have not taken action soon enough. We allow situations to continue until we blow up or give up. We give multiple warnings until we are out of control (which puts children in control). We finally scream in anger and the child finally moves. We then mistakenly think it is the anger that has worked but it is not the anger, however, it is the fact that we finally took action. Sound familiar? To reverse the situation and gain control, we must follow three principles.

Communication
Often when our children are irritating us we say such things as "Stop that" or "If you don't behave you are going to be in trouble." To gain control we need to sharpen our communication by *going to* the child, looking him in the eye and stating clearly what we want him to do and what the consequences will be if he does not comply. This should be done in not more than two or three sentences. "Johnny, I want you to turn off the TV now. If I have to remind you again you will not be allowed to watch TV for the rest of the week. Do you understand?" (Make sure you get a response.)

Do not get into an argument. If you do, your child wins and is in control. Simply repeat what you want him to do.

Action
If this does not work, there is a second step you must take. Follow through with the promised consequence of your child's misbehavior immediately. In the illustration given you would say, "Johnny, you have not turned off the TV so you have chosen to not watch TV for the rest of the week." Of course Johnny will argue but now is the time for the "broken record." Do not argue with him or he will be in control once again. Simply repeat, "Johnny, you did not

turn off the TV and you have chosen not to watch TV for the rest of the week."

Persistence

By persistence I mean following through with your plan. Make sure that you do steps one and two consistently and follow through with the consequences. If you fail to be persistent then your child will once again take control.

Wearing your C.A.P. takes practice and is not easy. But, the other option, your child being in control, will make the effort seem worthwhile.

Choosing the Right
Method of Discipline

Following are some situations that call for discipline. Choose a method of discipline and explain how you would use it.

Situtation 1. Johnny leaves his belongings strung out throughout the house. His bedroom is a mess. Johnny's mother and father find themselves either yelling at him or picking up his things. What methods of discipline should they use?

Situation 2. Amy has a habit of showing off and embarrassing her parents when the family entertains guests.

Situation 3. Sharon seldom comes home from playing when she is supposed to.

Situation 4. Tad has a habit of saying, "Gimme some bread," (or whatever other food he wants) at the table. Tad's parents correct him but he continues to have poor manners.

Situation 5. Josh, age eight, and Jason, age ten, are constantly arguing and fighting. Mom and Dad have tried reasoning, spanking and yelling. Nothing seems to work.

---

[1]*Anna B. Mow, Your Child.* Grand Rapids, MI: Zondervan Publishing House, 1963.

[2]*Dr. Bruce Narramore. An Ounce of Prevention.* Grand Rapids, MI: Zondervan Publishing House, 1973, pp. 76-85.

Discussion Questions

1. Give your definition of *discipline.*

2. Finish the sentence, "The most frustrating thing about discipling a child for me is ..."

3. In what ways could knowing the stages of morality be helpful to a parent?

4. Give an example of a child you have noticed (your own or someone else's) who has used one or more of the strategies of misbehavior.

5. Tell about a time when you became involved in a power struggle with your child.

6. The author lists seven methods of discipline: communication, negative reinforcement, positive reinforcement, extinction, natural consequences, logical consequences, and spanking. Rate these methods from 1—7 on how frequently you use them (1 for most frequently used, and so on.)

7. What do you think about "Time Out" as a regular method of discipline for children?

8. List two misbehaviors of your child that disturb you the most. Tell what method of discipline you now use. Is there a more suitable method?

9. The author gave five situations for which you were to choose methods of discipline. Be ready to share one of these.

10. After reading this chapter and evaluating myself, one thing I will change to improve my parenting is ...

CHAPTER 7

"I'm Glad to Be Me"

Believe it or not, almost every child development special-
ist and child psychologist agree upon one thing. The key to
a child's success in life is how he feels about himself—his
self-esteem. We want our children to accept themselves.

Think about yourself for a minute. Are you happy and
confident? Do you feel good about yourself, or do you have
real doubts about your self worth? Take just a moment
here and do a little project for me.

Finish the sentences on the next page that start with "I
am." Please write your answers in the blank spaces.

Now look at these statements about yourself. How many
of them are positive and how many are negative? If the
majority of your statements about yourself are positive
then chances are you have a good self-image. If more than
a third of the statements you made about yourself are negative than you could use a shot of self-esteem!

Most people who have low self-esteem learned to feel
poorly about themselves as they were growing up. The images we receive of ourselves from various people fit together to form an overall picture of ourselves. If these images are mostly positive, then chances are we will feel very
good about ourselves. If the images are largely negative
then our self-esteem will probably be low.

"I am _____."

"I am _____."

"I am _____."

"I am _____."

"I am _____."

"I am _____."

"I am _____."

"I am _____."

"I am _____."

"I am _____."

Our Need to Feel Loved and Accepted

Our self-esteem is tied closely to two great needs that God has placed in our lives. These are the needs to feel loved and accepted. The feedback that we receive from those whose opinions we feel are important largely determines whether these needs are fulfilled in our lives.

It is possible to feel loved and not feel accepted. When I was growing up I never doubted that my parents loved me. I did not, however, always feel accepted or worthwhile. The reason for this is that I felt that I was continually falling short of my parents' expectations. I was a "late bloomer" or an "underachiever," so school was always a hassle. Because I did not live up to the expectations of my parents and teachers I often felt that I was worthless. To compensate for these feelings of inferiority I became the class clown. Much to the dismay of my teachers, I did gain some notoriety. As I look back over my childhood and youth, I can see that a tremendous amount of my emotional energy was spent on trying to be accepted. It was only after I was married and made a commitment to Jesus Christ that I finally began to feel good about myself.

Helping Our Children Feel Good About Themselves

We all want our children to feel good about themselves. We want them to grow up to be confident successful adults. We can do some things as parents to help our children have good self-images, but we are not entirely responsible for their self-images, because life is complex and children are complex. Many things contribute to our children's feelings about themselves. For one thing, children's temperaments vary. If you have several children, you are probably aware that one child is naturally more self-assured than the others. Why? You have tried to give them equal love, attention, and acceptance. One child may seem completely confident of your love and acceptance of him and the other needs constant reassurance. One reason is that they are simply different persons with different needs. You had nothing to do with that. It is simply the way they were created.

In our family we have three girls. We have tried to show equal love and acceptance to all three. Two of our girls seem to have positive feelings about themselves. We have one daughter who struggles with her self-esteem. It is interesting that her basic temperament is very similar to mine. Some of us just have a more difficult time with our self-esteem than do others.

Children	Self-esteem Rate
	low medium high
Child #1 _____	1-2-3-4-5-6-7-8-9-10
Child #2 _____	1-2-3-4-5-6-7-8-9-10
Child #3 _____	1-2-3-4-5-6-7-8-9-10

How does your child feel about himself? Even though your children are very young, they are already giving you an indication of how they feel about themselves. Think about each of your children and rate each one's self-esteem on the scale on the previous page.

As parents, we can have a tremendous influence on our child's self-esteem. Think of yourself as a mirror that reflects back to your child, who he is and what he is worth. You are not the only mirror in his life, but you are the most important one. Your child's first images of his worth come through his senses in the first few months of his life. You bring your baby home from the hospital. He seems very unresponsive those first few weeks, but he is already building an image of himself. He feels your touch. He knows you can make him feel comfortable. He knows whether you are concerned about his hunger or not. He senses that you delight in him by your face and the way you talk to him. In those early months he is already beginning to know that he is a valued person—the beginnings of positive self-esteem. Soon he begins to understand words. These words reflect whether or not he is worthwhile. If he hears many positive statements about himself, he begins to see himself as worthwhile. If he hears constant negative statements, he begins to doubt his worth.

Parental Mirrors

You are your children's most important mirror. Throughout his life you will be giving reflections to him of his self worth. In Figure 7-1 you will find a mirror that shows the various ways we reflect to your child whether or not he is valued. The outside rim of the mirror represents influences other than ourselves. The inside of the mirror indicates the various ways that we, as parents, directly influence our child's self-esteem. As you look at this mirror, you may find areas in which you are not giving positive reflections to your children. These are areas in which you can improve. As we talk about each "reflection" of the mirror, make a plus by the areas in which you reflect a positive self-image

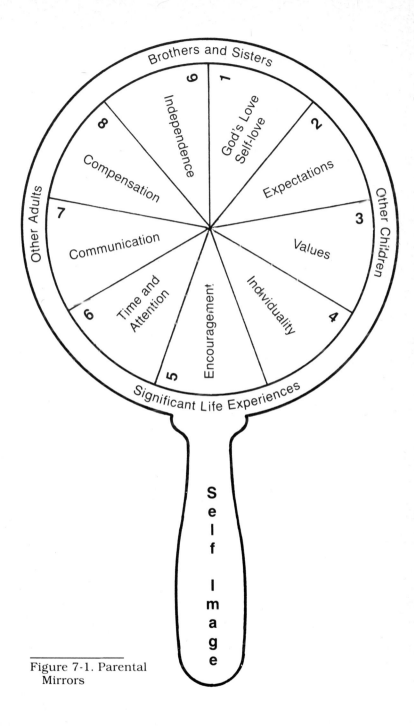

Figure 7-1. Parental
Mirrors

to your children, and a minus by the areas in which you reflect a negative self-image. When you have finished this chapter, choose one or two areas to work on.

Let's take a look at outside factors that influence your child's self-esteem. First there are your child's *brothers and sisters.* Whether your child feels accepted by his brothers and sisters can affect his entire life. My father's brother, who had superior intelligence and creativity, used to refer to my father as "Dumb Don" when they were growing up. I believe that my father wore the scars of those remarks his entire life. He did achieve, but the damage done to his self-esteem was evident.

Children do not realize the power they have to build or destroy their brothers and sisters self-esteem. It is awesome. We have talked to our older girls many times about their attitude toward their "bratty" little sister. Bridget longs for their approval, but it seems like she seldom gets it. We once listed some feeling statements during a Family Night and Bridget said, "I feel good about myself when Heidi and Liesl treat me nice." She hurriedly added that it never happened.

One hard and fast rule in our home is that our girls are *never* allowed to make remarks about the others physical appearance. It sometimes happens, but it is a family rule that we strive to enforce. Remarks about another person's appearance, even when it is supposedly done in jest, can be destructive to a person's self-esteem. Parents should never allow it to happen.

Another reflection from outside the home that influences the way our children feel about themselves is *other children.* This can be a strong influence. Children need an adequate amount of positive feedback from their peers to feel good about themselves. This usually involves achievement in areas that your child's peer group feels is important. This fact hit us a few years ago when we moved to Napa, California. Bridget enrolled in a new school and soon started complaining that the teacher and classmates did not like her. As time went on, she would say, "No one likes me." I thought she was exaggerating. She had never had problems with her peers before, so I thought it was just her imagination or an adjustment problem. The first session we had with her teacher helped us put the picture together. The teacher did not like Bridget, and her modeling had turned the entire class against her. The teacher said to my wife and me, "Do you know that no one in this class likes Bridget?" As you can imagine, Bridget had a horrible year. Her self-esteem was at an all time low. Janet and I were extremely concerned. We finally pulled Bridget out of that class and even considered moving her to a different school. It took her almost a full year to work out her peer problems, but by the time she was a sixth grader in that same school she considered herself one of the most popular girls. Her self-esteem was much higher. Other children and other adults do have power to build or tear down our children's self-esteem. We need to monitor these relationships. I am not advocating stepping in, except in case of grave concern, but do be alert to the possible dangers.

Other influences on your child's self-esteem are *other adults* and *significant life experiences*.

Reflection 1: God's Love/Self-love

How do you feel about yourself? This is an important question to ask, for it is very difficult to give positive reflections to your children if you have not first come to grips with your self-esteem. We all have periods of low self-esteem, but as a general rule, how do you feel about yourself? To feel good about others and help them see their worth, we must feel good about ourselves and see our worth.

I began to develop a positive self-image when I made a commitment to Christ. I began to understand the real meaning of being a child of God. *I had a heavenly Father that was king of the universe* (John 1:12, Galatians 4:4-6). I was made in the image of God, which meant I reflected some of the character of God. God was personally interested in me and had a distinct plan for my life. I was so important to God that He was willing to send His own Son to die for me. "I must be important," I thought. These nuggets of truth changed the entire direction of my life. I committed my life to Jesus when I was twenty-nine. At that time I was a construction laborer with a wife and two children. I had very little confidence in myself. Eight years later I had graduated from college and seminary and had published my first book. What was the change? I now had a growing confidence that from God's perspective I was a person of great worth and that He had a special plan for my life. That is true of each one of you. If you have doubts about yourself, start looking at yourself from God's point of view. An excellent book to help you improve your self-image is *You're Someone Special* by Bruce Narramore (Zondervan).

Reflection 2: Expectations

We all have expectations for our children. We need to ask ourselves these questions: Are these expectations realistic? Are they unselfish? How do they affect our children?

I remember the tremendous pressure I put on Heidi, our oldest girl, when she was about three or four. She was going to be a genius. I was going to make sure she read by the age of four. Poor kid! My expectations for her were not reasonable and were selfish. I was trying to live my life through her. Because I never achieved at school, I was going to achieve through her. As parents we need to be especially careful that our expectations are not just making our children extensions of our own personalities.

Sometimes it may appear that we are doing what is best for our children but the results are detrimental to their self-esteem. We want our children to take music lessons. We rationalize that this is best for them. "Music will enrich my child's life. I didn't have such a chance but my child will." The problem may be that your child has no interest in music. He resents taking music lessons but he wants to please you. He wants to do what you expect. Many times the results are family hassles and lowered self-esteem on the part of the child.

Sometimes our expectations for grades can be a big problem. Who says a child must have "A's"? What is wrong with average grades? A child's self-esteem can suffer if he feels that he is continually falling short of his parent's expectations in school. Of course, reasonable expectations are necessary. We need to challenge our children to live up to their potential. The question we need to ask ourself is, are our expectations reasonable or are they too high? Do we want our children to do well in school for their good, or to make us feel good about being "super parents."

Expecting too much from children *at too early an age* can also damage self-esteem. Expecting a three-year-old to gladly share his toys and to be neat and tidy, can chip away at self-esteem. Children think, "I'm never good enough."

There is a balance we need to work toward here. That balance is reasonable expectations that are compatible with the age of our children.

Reflection 3: Values

As Christian parents we must be careful that we do not communicate a worldly value system to our children. Things like outer beauty, intelligence, athletic ability, social status, power and material wealth, make up what the world considers important. God's values are opposite to these. God stressed inner beauty—"But the Lord said to Samuel, 'Do not look at his appearance or at the height of his stature, because I have rejected him; for God sees not as man sees, for man looks at the outward appearance, but the Lord looks at the heart'" (1 Samuel 16:7). Intelligence was not especially important to God either. In 1 Corinthians 1:26 Paul says, "For consider your calling, brethren, that there were not many wise according to the flesh, not many mighty, not many noble."

In 1 Timothy 4:8 Paul compares the value of bodily exercise with godliness. Godliness wins out because it offers "promise for the present life and also for the life to come." What about power and prestige? Jesus had something to say to his disciples about that: "Let him who is the greatest among you become as the youngest, and the leader as the servant" (Luke 22:26). The Bible is full of warnings about over emphasis on material possessions. Paul warns about the temptations of money in 1 Timothy 6:10 when he says, "For the love of money is a root of all sorts of evil."

It is clear that God's values are not man's values, but what has this to do with your child's self-esteem? Let me answer this by asking some questions. If your child has average looks, what happens to his feelings about himself when he sees you talking about children who are "beautiful"? How does a child feel without athletic ability about himself when a father raves about the athletic gifts of other boys? How does a child with average intelligence feel when other children with superior mental capabilities are singled out as the "neat kids."

We need to be especially careful to communicate godly values to our children. They are very aware of our values and when they do not measure up in these areas, self-esteem can be damaged.

Reflection 4: Individuality

It hurts to be compared to someone else and yet most parents fall into the trap of comparing their child unfavorably with brothers, sisters or other children. This can be a real blow to a child's self-esteem and is really unnecessary. Each child is a special creation of God—a unique individual, the only one of his kind.

> For Thou didst form my inward parts;
> Thou didst weave me in my mother's womb.
> I will give thanks to Thee, for I am fearfully
>   and wonderfully made;
> Wonderful are Thy works,
> And my soul knows it very well.
>   —Psalm 139:13, 14

Every child should feel he is a unique creation of His heavenly Father. That there is no one just like him. Look for the things in your child that make him different and precious. Even weaknesses are many times strengths in disguise. Talk to your child often about how he is special. I was talking to Bridget about her uniqueness one night— praising some of her neat qualities.

"Oh, Dad," she said, embarrassed, "why do you do that?"

"Okay, I'll stop," I replied.

"No, it's okay, Dad," she replied quickly. "Go on."

Reflection 5: Encouragement

If our children are going to really believe in themselves and have a good self-image, they must have encouragement from us. Scripture tells us to, "Encourage one another, and build up one another, just as you also are doing" (1 Thessalonians 5:11). Children are people too and need encouragement. Sometimes we become so involved in the negative—pick that up, be quiet, don't fight, clean your room, eat your food—that we forget to focus on the assets and strengths in our child's life. They can become discouraged by too much negative input. They can begin to feel that they are not worthwhile.

Make it a point every day to encourage your child in some area. Encourage the effort or the improvement your child is making. When you focus on his good points, he will want to do better. If we focus on our child's weak points, he will become discouraged and not even try. We need to accept *our children as they are*, not only as what we want them to become. *People seldom improve unless they feel good enough about themselves to believe they can improve.*

Reflection 6: Time and Attention

When you spend *time* with someone it says, "You are important." Spending time is an esteem builder. When you give someone your undivided *attention*, that also says, "You are important." Spending quality time with your child is *essential* to his self-image. Not spending time with your child says, "You are not important." You may be a parent that doesn't have a lot of spare time. Join the crowd. Few of us do. But you can still carve out nuggets of time for your children. It's not always the amount of time that we spend with our children but what we do with the time. If you are a father, when you come home at night, make contact with your child right away. Just a few minutes of conversation will make him feel important. Later in the evening you could spend some time wrestling with him or reading him a book. You initiate the time together—don't always wait for your child to approach you.

You might be a woman who is spending all day with a preschool child. Sometimes this situation makes it even more difficult to have quality time. A self-centered two- or three-year-old will take *all* your time if you let him. On the other hand, it is possible to get so wrapped up in cleaning the house and the negative aspects of disciplining the child that you seldom spend quality time together. Single out some time each day that you are not going to worry about the house or your child's behavior. You are going to just focus on him and have a good time. This will mean the TV is off, the newspaper is laid down and there are just the two of you—building relationships.

Reflection 7: Communication

Loving communication builds self-esteem. Words have tremendous power of building or tearing down. One thing we always need to do is separate the deed from the doer in our communication. Children many times fall short of our expectations. We must always let them know that they are loved and valued no matter how they are *performing* at the time. We must be careful of communication that causes the child to feel that he is a worthless person.

Judgment language such as, "You are a bad girl," or "You are a lazy child," fails to separate the deed from the doer and is destructive to a child's self-esteem. A parent can still communicate displeasure with behavior without labeling the child as "bad" or "lazy" or "messy." This can be done with feeling statements such as, "I feel frustrated when I ask you to clean your room and it is still a mess." In this communication you are focusing on the behavior and not attacking the character of the child.

Reflection 8: Compensation

We have Dr. James Dobson to thank for this insight. In his excellent book on self-esteem, *Hide or Seek*, Dobson suggests that parents help their children capitalize on their strengths, which counterbalance their weaknesses. This means looking for something your children have the potential to do well and helping them excel in that area. A child might be poorly coordinated and not do well in sports, but be able to excel in playing a musical instrument. A child might do poorly in some aspects of school but excel in one area, such as writing stories or drawing. Look closely at your child and determine an area of compensation. Do everything in your power to help him develop this area in his life. This can be a great boost to his self-esteem.

Reflection 9: Independence

Stage number two of the stages of growth was "developing a sense of autonomy," of independence. Visualize a two-year-old demanding, "Me do," as he tries to pull on his socks. What happens when the parents keep stepping in and doing things for the child? What happens when his drive for independence is thwarted? The child learns to think of himself as inadequate. Low self-esteem is the inevitable result of the child whose parents overprotect him or in other ways hamper his drive for independence. We should allow our young children lots of room to grow and develop, even if it is frustrating for us. Our frustration is a small price to pay for an independent child who feels good about himself.

Conclusion

Which reflection of the parental mirror do you need to work on? Choose one to start working on this week. One of the greatest gifts we can give our children is helping them build a positive self-image.

Discussion Questions

1. When you were growing up, what positive or negative effects did your parents have on your self-esteem?

2. The author states that it is possible to feel loved but not accepted. Do you agree or disagree with this statement? Why or why not?

3. Give a brief statement about how you think your child feels about himself and how you rated him on the scale of 1—10.

4. The author mentions several influences other than parents on a child's self-esteem. Which one do you think is the greatest? Why?

5. Make a list of five expectations you have for your children. Put an "R" by those you feel are realistic, an "S" by those that involve selfish ambitions of your own and a "U" by those you feel *might* be unrealistic. How do you see these expectations influencing your children?

6. Make a list of the unique characteristics of your child (children). What makes him special to you?

7. On a scale of 1—10, rate how well you encourage your child.

8. Write a statement about the *quantity* and *quality* of time you spend with your child.

9. Of the nine "reflections" described above, which do you need to work on the most?

10. After reading this chapter and evaluating myself, one thing I will change about my parenting is ...

CHAPTER 8

"I'm Listening!"

"I hate my teacher!" says seven-year-old Amber, with tears streaming down her face.

"Now Amber," replies mother, "you know that you love your teacher. How can you say something like that?"

What we have here is a classic breakdown in communication between a school child and her parent. Amber, in this situation, was sharing her feelings of "ambivalence." In other words, Amber was feeling love and intense dislike for her teacher at the same time. At this moment, however, the feelings of dislike, because of something that had happened that day, were much more intense than the feelings of love. Amber's mother did not understand her daughter's communication, and denied her feelings. As a result, Amber felt confused and misunderstood.

Here is another example of poor communication with a young child. Your four-year-old child comes home from playing with a friend next door. With tear-filled eyes he says, "Tommy hates me. He doesn't ever want to play with me again. I won't have anyone to play with."

"That's silly," you reply to your son, "Tommy really doesn't hate you, he's just mad. He will play with you in a little while."

While all you have said may be true, you have just blown

communication with your son because he hasn't heard what you have said. He does not think his feelings have been heard, so he has closed his ears to what you have to say.

Good communication involves three principles given in Scripture. "Let every one be quick to hear, slow to speak and slow to anger; for the anger of man does not achieve the righteousness of God" (James 1:19, 20).

These principles are really skills that we can develop. The first skill is slow speech, which involves expressing our feelings carefully. The second skill given in this Scripture passage is what I call "reflective listening." This involves listening beyond the words, to what the person really feels. The third skill is to control anger. We will be dealing with these three skills in this chapter. First a thought about the importance of listening.

Listening always involves looking behind the words to the real intent of the message. Words are only part of the communication process. Think of the communication between you and your spouse as an example. You have had a horrendous day with your two preschool children. They have terrorized you all day after you had been up with them three times the night before. You are sick of kids and thoroughly exhausted. You have just barely managed to stay sane until your husband arrives home. He walks in the door and you unload. "These kids are absolute monsters. They have refused to obey me all day long. I've had it. I don't know what I'm going to do."

Your husband seems concerned about the situation and a little annoyed. "Let's sit down and talk about it," he says. "I've been noticing that you haven't been very consistent with the children lately. I don't think the kids are ever going to obey you until you start being consistent in your discipline."

Your response is anything but that of the gentle Christian wife. You stomp off in a rage with your husband following you saying, "What did I say? I was only trying to help."

But help he did not. Why? Because you had some intense feelings and he passed those by to go directly to problem solving. You did not need that kind of help. You were very well aware of consistency and the other finer points of dis-

112

cipline. What you did need was for your husband to put his arms around you and in some way acknowledge your feelings, if nothing more than by saying, "You must have had a horrible day."

Learning the Language of Feelings

If we are to communicate effectively with our school children, we must learn the language of feelings. The language of feelings is as natural as life itself. It is part of the "original equipment" that God gifted us with. The problem is that, in our own childhood, we probably did not really learn how to use this language.

When we were very young, we learned through trial and error which feelings were appropriate to express and which were not. We quickly discovered that if we crawled up on our parent's lap and said, "I love you," that our parents responded to us in a very positive way. But we also had other feelings inside of us that we expressed. Feelings like, "I hate you," when we were feeling angry towards someone. We were either denied the feeling—"You really don't hate your brother"—or we were told never to say "ugly" things like that again. We were marched into our brother's room where we were told to say, "I'm sorry I said, 'I hate you,'" when we were still angry and not sorry at all.

The school of feelings went on. We learned that it was unwise to say what we really felt about food at the table, or how we felt about clothes that our mother bought us. We also realized that it was much easier to say "Yes" when our mother asked, "Brad, please let your cousin play with your truck," than to say "No" and be ashamed by the sermon on sharing again.

Feelings Are a Gift From God
Our first step in learning the language of feelings is accepting that our feelings are a gift from God. It is not hard for most Christians to accept their positive feelings as a gift from God, but many people feel the negative feelings are directly from Satan.

113

God has gifted us with a full range of feelings, both positive and negative. These feelings are neither good nor bad. They have no morality. It is what we do with these feelings—our actions—that are good or bad. There is a difference, for example, between angry feelings and angry actions.

Jesus experienced the full range of feelings and did not sin. In Mark 3:1-5, we find the Pharisees watching Jesus in the synagogue to see if He would heal a man with a withered hand on the Sabbath. Jesus knew their thoughts and became *angry;* "After looking around at them with anger, grieved at their hardness of heart, He said to the man, 'Stretch out your hand,' and he stretched it out, and his hand was restored."

The Scriptures say that Jesus was troubled, and that He wept over the death of His close friend, Lazarus (John 11:33-35). At the Mount of Olives, we find Jesus grieved and distressed, calling upon God to "let this cup pass from Me, yet not as I will, but as Thou wilt" (Matthew 26:36-39).

Jesus, in all of these cases, experienced what we would call negative feelings, but He did not sin. Why? Because when the feeling came, He made the appropriate response. God never holds us accountable for our feelings, only what we do with our feelings, our actions.

Becoming Aware of Our Feelings

Communication involves two important aspects of the language of feelings: sharing your own feelings and responding to the feelings of others. If we are not aware of how we are feeling, we will have great difficulty responding to the feelings of our children.

Awareness comes by allowing ourselves to feel (accepting our feelings as a gift from God) and examining our feelings. Many times we concentrate on *what we think* so much, that we fail to bring *how we feel* into balance. How often do you stop and think, "What is that feeling that I am experiencing right now?"

You come home from work after having a tremendous amount of pressure from the boss to meet a deadline. You made it, but you have had it. You get home and your children are glad to see you. They are also a little hyper. You begin screaming at them to be quiet. Your wife gets on your back for being so harsh on them. You get angry and go out to your garage to work with things that don't give you flack.

A lot of misunderstandings could have been avoided if you had been aware of your feelings and communicated them to your family. What were you feeling? You might have been feeling very nervous from all the pressure you had that day. You might have been feeling angry at your boss for putting the pressure on you. You might have just been frustrated with the whole situation.

When you become aware of those feelings you can handle your situations much easier. For example, if you were aware of being nervous, you could have communicated that to your wife and children by saying, "I had a really bad day at work. I'm really nervous and the noise is driving me crazy. I think I need to go out and work in the garage for a while." When you understand your own feelings, you avoid venting your frustrations on your wife and children. By doing this you prevent unnecessary conflict.

On the list below, make a check by the feelings that you experience often. Make an "o" by the feelings you rarely experience. Make an exclamation point by the feelings you experience with great intensity.

Feelings Awareness List

accepted	dependent	impatient
affectionate	disappointed	inadequate
afraid	dominated	incompetent
angry	domineering	in control
anxious	eager to please	inferior
appreciated	embarrassed	inhibited
attractive	envious	insecure
calm	excited	jealous
closed	frustrated	lonely
competent	guilty	lovable
confused	happy	optimistic
creative	hostile	pessimistic
cut off from others	hurt	phony
defeated	ignored	possessive

Reflective Listening

When you are aware of your own feelings, you can develop the essential skill of reflective listening. Reflective listening is letting your school child know that you are aware of the feelings behind what he is saying and not saying.

We all are aware that a child who is experiencing strong feelings does not listen to advice or constructive criticism. He tends to lose perspective. By listening reflectively, we help our child feel understood and we help him clarify his feelings. Reflective listening involves grasping what the child feels and means, and then stating the meaning so the child feels understood and accepted. *Reflective listening provides a sort of mirror for the child to see himself or herself more clearly.* In other words, it gives the child "feedback."[1]

For an example of non-reflective listening, let's think of seven-year-old Amber again. When Amber came home upset about school and said, "I hate my teacher!" Mother's reply was, "Now Amber, you know that you love your teacher. How can you say something like that?" Amber's mother did not accept her daughter's feelings, nor did she listen reflectively. In fact, she told Amber that she was not feeling that way and reprimanded her for saying that she had that feeling. Amber learned very little from that encounter except that feelings of dislike are inappropriate.

If Amber's mother was listening reflectively, she might have responded by saying, "You seem to be very angry at your teacher right now." In this case, Amber's mother has indicated to her that she has heard the feelings behind the words. Because of this, Amber will probably keep talking and tell her mother what happened. After Amber shares more information, then Amber's mother will be able to help her work through her feelings and resolve the problem. The rule of reflective listening is, "that statements of understanding *precede* statements of advice or instruction."[2] Many of us are locked into the opposite of this. I recently held a seminar on communication for a group of preschool parents. I went over the principles of reflective listening that I have just shared with you. I then put the parents in groups and gave them a list of children's statements to which they were to respond by listening reflectively. As I visited each group, I found that they all had one thing in common. Each group was trying to solve the children's problems rather than responding to the feelings by reflective listening. They had missed the whole point. The reason for this is that most of us have the habit of trying to resolve the problem when our child shares a strong emotion with us before we identify with the feelings. Our procedure looks something like this for non-reflective listening.

Child shares feeling: Parent argues against feeling.
Parent tries to solve problem.

When a parent uses reflective listening, the procedure looks different.

Child shares feeling: Parent accepts feeling.
Parent works toward solution.

The following are some typical statements of children followed by two responses by parents. One of the responses is reflective listening and the other is not.

Statement by child: "I wish Jimmy would go somewhere else to live" (Jimmy is the younger brother).

Response number 1: "That's a terrible thing to say about your brother. Go to your room and wait for me."
Response number 2: "You sound like you are very angry at your brother right now."

Which of the two responses were reflective listening? Response number 2 identified with the child's feelings and opened the door formore discussion about the problem.

Statement by child: "I'm never going to go outside and play again. Billy's mean."

Response number 1: "It sounds like you are afraid that Billy will pick on you."
Response number 2: "Don't be silly. Go outside and play. Billy's a nice boy."

Response number 1 is reflective listening. This response lets Billy know that his feelings have been heard.

Here is an exercise that will help you develop reflective listening. There are six statements by children. Write a reflective listening response sentence for each one.

Statement by child: "Why can't I go across the street? You
   never let me do anything."

   Your response _____

   _____

Statement by child: "I don't like that baby sitter. She picks
   on me."

   Your response _____

   _____

Statement by child: "I hate Bobby. He's no good." *(Bobby is
   a younger brother.)*

   Your response _____

   _____

Statement by child: "I'm going to run away from home.
   You don't love me."

   Your response _____

   _____

Statement by child: "You are the meanest mother in the
   world."

   Your response _____

   _____

Statement by child: "I can't do it."

Your response _____

_____

Expressing Your Feelings

Your five-year-old child has destroyed the house for the sixth straight day. You are knee deep in toys and furious. The question is, how are you going to express those feelings of anger to your child so that they are understood? The best way to express feelings, even to a preschool child, is to use "I-messages." A "you-message" is usually not heard because it lays blame. Now, of course, your child has certainly contributed to your misery, but you do want to be heard. An "I-message" lets your child know his behavior is affecting you. With an "I-message" you have a much better chance of being heard.

Here is an example of the two types of messages. First the "you-message." Your five-year-old has cluttered the house with toys. You say, "You make me so mad. You are the messiest kid I've ever seen." In this message, you have expressed your feelings, but your child is not going to listen. He heard the word "you" and tuned you out. An "I-message" in the same situation would go something like this: "I feel angry when toys are left all over the house because I like the house to be clean." In the last statement your child will be more apt to hear your feelings because you have shared how you feel. He will not be as defensive. You have been specific about how his behavior is affecting you. Of course, if that "I-message" is expressed with a high level of hostility, it will not be heard. We do need to be in control of our anger when we express feelings to our children.

Construct "I-messages" of some feelings that you have had this week. Start your message with "I-feel," and then state your feeling. Next add "when" and describe the situation. Complete your "I-message" with the word "because." This helps you share what's happening to you because of the situation.

Let's look at another "I-message" and see how the three parts fit together. You have a friend over and your child keeps interrupting. You say, "I *feel* annoyed *when* I keep getting interrupted *because* it's very difficult to carry on a conversation."

Now it's your turn to formulate some "I-messages." Think of two reccurring situations that happen in your home. Use the "I-message" formula to express how you feel.

Situation 1—_____ .

"I feel _____ when _____

_____ , because _____

_____."

Situation 2—_____ .

"I feel _____ when _____

_____

because _____."

What to Expect

I would like to share a final word about expectations— what to expect from yourself and what to expect from your child when you are listening reflectively and sending "I-messages."

First of all, it takes a long time to be skillful at listening to feelings and sharing feelings. Secondly, you will find yourself using your skills only part of the time. No parent that I know of always responds to their children with reflective listening. That is just not realistic. We are human beings with our own emotions and hangups. There are times when we simply choose not to communicate in productive ways. Don't discourage yourself by trying to be the "perfect parent." If you use *some* of the skills you have learned in this chapter *some* of the time, you are going to be a good communicating parent.

Your children are human too. Sometimes they will respond to your reflective listening and sometimes they will not. Sometimes they will hear your "I-messages" and sometimes you'll wonder if all this work is worth it.

Your very young children will do very little responding to the skills we have been talking about. Some of you with two-year-olds have probably been trying to visualize using these skills with your child. Two-year-olds communicate on their level and have no interest in your "reflective listening" or "I-message" skills. As your children reach three, four and five, you will see them gradually responding to these methods of communication. They will learn as you learn. Learning skills of "reflective listening" and I-messages" will enrich your relationship with your children.

---

[1]Don Dinkmeyer and Gary D. McKay, *Parent's Handbook.* Circle Pines, MN: AGS, 1976, p. 47.

[2]Dr. Haim Ginott, *Between Parent and Child.* New York: Macmillan, 1965, p. 25.

Discussion Questions

1. Describe how you communicate with your child now. What works for you? What doesn't work?

2. When you were growing up, how were the expressions of feelings encouraged or discouraged?

3. How do you feel when someone does not pick up on how you feel and tries to "solve" your problem?

4. "Feelings are neither good nor bad. They have no morality." What do you think about that statement?

5. On a scale of 1—10, how aware are you of your feelings?

6. In your own words, share the strengths or weaknesses of reflective listening.

7. Be ready to share one of your "reflective listening" responses from pp. 118-9.

8. What do you find is the most difficult part of expressing your feelings in "I-messages"?

9. Be ready to share an "I-message."

10. After reading this chapter and evaluating myself, one thing I will change to improve my parenting is ...

Section 3

What to Do When Your Children Fight

CHAPTER 9

Why Do Brothers and Sisters Fight?

"At last," you think, "some peace and quiet," as you settle down with your magazine. Then it happens again. A bloodcurdling scream from the children's bedroom. "He hit me!" comes the agonized voice of a wounded child. You tear down the hall to your children's bedroom to view what you are sure will be a battered and bleeding child. Instead, your children are sulking in opposite corners of the room, both seemingly unmarked.

"OK, let's hear it," you say angrily, "what's going on?"

"Jason hit me for no reason," says your nine-year-old son, Curt.

"That's not true," says your seven-year-old son, Jason. "He wouldn't give me my truck back. That's why I hit him."

"But he said I could play with the truck today if I would let him go to the store with me."

You quickly find yourself being a judge in the affair, trying to make some sense of the jumbled mess of accusations and counteraccusations. "How is it possible to know who is really to blame?" you ask yourself. "Why can't my children get along like children in other families I know? I hate this fighting. It tears me apart to see my children fighting like this."

Change the scene to home number two. Loud arguing is coming from the vicinity of the hall bathroom. As you move in close to see what is going on, you hear the words you dread. "I hate you Wendy. You think you are so perfect. Just stay away. I don't even want to talk to you." *Hate*—the word penetrates deeply into your emotions. Does Debbie really hate her sister? What a terrible word! What a horrible feeling for a Christian teenager to have for her sister!

You are hurt that your children could have such ungodly feelings for one another. "How could I have failed so miserably as a parent?" you ask yourself. You remember the earlier years when they fought, but they also seemed to have much love for one another. Now as teenagers, there seems to be real bitterness developing at a time when you thought they would be becoming best friends. You are at the end of your rope. You don't know what to do.

What can you do about the sibling rivalry that almost certainly exists in some form within your family? If you are like most parents I talk to, you are concerned about the way your children get along with one another. You are vitally interested in teaching your children the essential Christian attribute of loving one another. This is rightfully so, for this is what Jesus said the Christian life is all about.

You do not have to sit helplessly by as your children rip each other apart, either physically or emotionally. This is, however, a difficult subject, so there are no easy answers. It is possible to help your children have a better understanding of themselves, of one another, and of how God wants them to love one another. The first step to helping your children is to remember how it was for you when you were a sibling.

Evaluation of My
Sibling Relationships

"Me, Fight With My Brothers and Sisters?"

To get in touch with what our children are going through with their brothers and sisters, we must get in touch with our own family background. Think back to your childhood for a few minutes. The following evaluation form will help you recapture some of your own feelings when you were growing up and enable you to better understand your children's struggles with their brothers and sisters. Apply all questions and open-ended statements to your own sibling relationships.

What is the strongest emotion you experience when you think back to your relationship with your brothers and sisters? Circle one. What is the second strongest?

love   jealousy   hate   rejections   happiness   warmth

I realize that your relationship with each brother and sister was different. You may want to qualify your answers by rating your relationship with each brother and sister separately.

Complete the following open-ended sentences:

I wish my mother and father had understood _____

_____

My parents handled sibling relationships _____

_____

I secretly wished _____

_____

The greatest hurt I had as a sibling was _____

_____

If my parents had known how I felt, they would have ____

_____

_____

Even now, I sometimes feel _____

The most difficult aspect of being a sibling for me was ___

_____

What is different about your relationship with your brothers and sisters now, as compared to when you were growing up?

_____

_____

Evaluate your relationship with your brothers and sisters when you were growing up and now. Circle one.

Growing up: terrible   fair   good   excellent

Now: terrible   fair   good   excellent

Use stick figures to place your brothers and sisters in emotional distance to yourself when your were growing up.

Place yourself and your brothers and sisters in emotional distance to your mother and father.

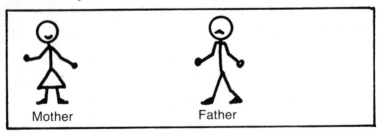

Figure 9-1. Sibling Relationships

A Letter to Your Parents

Relax! This is a letter that you will never mail. Write a letter to your parents telling them your needs as a sibling, and sharing how you would have liked sibling relationships to have been handled in your family.

Dear Mom and Dad,

For some of you, this evaluation has been an emotional experience. It has stirred up old feelings that may have been dormant for some time. Perhaps you were the scapegoat of the family, on whom everyone, it seemed, dumped their anger. You might have been a second child, always trying to keep up with the firstborn. If you were raised in a family where children were compared, you might have left-over feelings of resentment, or you may still be competing with brothers and sisters for your parents' approval. Many will experience ambivalent feelings—that is opposite feelings at the same time—such as love and resentment. Some of you may have been "only children," so you have been able to observe the feelings of sibling rivalry only by watching other children and your own. Still others were raised in homes where there was a minimum of sibling rivalry. Whatever your situation, I hope you are seeing the difficulties that come with the privilege of being a sibling.

Managing Sibling Rivalry

Being a parent of a sibling is also difficult. We need to understand three basic concepts.

Sibling Rivalry Is Natural

In the earliest accounts of man, sibling rivalry is introduced to us in a most dramatic and tragic way. Adam and

129

Eve sinned and were expelled from the Garden of Eden. In chapter four of Genesis, the story is told of Cain and Abel, the first recorded children of Adam and Eve. Abel was a keeper of flocks, and Cain was a tiller of the ground. We read nothing about the child rearing practices of the parents, but we do read of the deep jealousy and hate that developed between the brothers. Abel's offering to the Lord was acceptable but Cain's was not. Cain, in a fit of jealousy, killed his brother. That is sibling rivalry at its worst.

Sibling rivalry is natural because of the intrusion of sin on our character. Through Adam and Eve, sin was introduced into the world and thus each of us have sinful natures (Romans 3:23). Like Cain, we are self-seeking. In our own selfish ways, we want to be number one. If as adults we have trouble with our selfishness, think of how difficult it must be for our children. *They each secretly want to be number one in our eyes.* They want to be the favorite. It is extremely important to remember this fact. It is natural for a child to wish he was first in your attention and affection. It is not his greatest delight to willingly share you with his brothers and sisters, so don't expect a great deal of self-sacrificing in this area. Expect some competition for your attention and affection. *Remember you are the greatest prize.* It is you that they want the exclusive rights to. The word *rivalry* actually means "using the same stream as another." During the frontier days there were fights, even murders over the use of streams. You are the source of a stream of emotions that each of your children have equal rights to. Expect some competition for those emotions.

Sibling Rivalry Is Not All Bad

It is a temptation for us to write off all our children's fights and squabbles as being bad. This is not necessarily so. It is frustrating when our children are not getting along. The constant (so it seems) bickering is aggravating. Believe it or not, some good can result from this sibling rivalry. Your children are learning to resolve conflict. It is within the home, and specifically between brothers and sisters, that the skills of settling differences can be learned. Admittedly, this does take supervision. The skills are learned over a long period of time, but they are being learned. Management of conflict is essential and we will deal with it in a later chapter.

Another positive aspect of sibling rivalry is that it serves as a buffer between the child and the cruel world outside the home. Think of the child who has experienced only positive emotions in his home. He does not have brothers and sister to compete (fight) with. His parents are loving, nurturing people. Then the little guy goes to school for the first time. Welcome to the real world, fellow! It's tough out there. Children can be pretty cruel at times. Being sensitive to the feelings of their peers is not their strong suit! Watch the give-and-take on a playground or listen to groups that shut other kids out. It can be devastating to a child who has not been exposed to some of the real world in his own home. The give-and-take with brothers and sisters toughens the child for life.

Sibling Rivalry Must Be Managed

Parents seem to adopt two extremes when it comes to managing sibling rivalry—some overmanage and some undermanage. Those who overmanage step into fights too soon and the children fail to learn how to resolve conflict and manage their own behavior. The other extreme is to ignore what is going on. Both extremes are potentially disastrous. Most of us fall somewhere between the two extremes. Managing sibling rivalry involves gaining a balance between the two.

We cannot take the problem of sibling rivalry too lightly. History is strewn with damaged emotions caused by mismanaged sibling relationships.

My father, for example was a victim of sibling rivalry mismanagement when he was growing up. He had an extremely gifted older brother who delighted in calling him "Dumb Don." The constant belittling of my father had a lasting effect on his self-image. Although my father was a bright man who succeeded in the pastoral ministry and mission work, he always lacked confidence in himself. It was as if he still heard the voice of his brother saying "Dumb Don."

Where were my dad's parents when all this was going on? They were simply not aware of the damaging effects

131

that one sibling can have on another. They were not aware that damaging words can haunt a person for years. My grandparents were fine Christian people who loved their children. They had simply mismanaged sibling rivalry.

Our responsibility as parents is to understand sibling rivalry and its power for good and bad. This understanding should enable us to manage the sibling rivalry in our home.

Discussion Questions

1. What emotions do you experience when your children are not getting along with one another?

2. What is most difficult for you to cope with when your children fight with one another?

3. What is the strongest emotion you experience when you think back to your relationship with your brothers and sisters? Explain.

4. Where were you in the birth order of your family (oldest, a middle child, youngest)? How did you feel about your position in the family?

5. What do you wish your parents had known about sibling rivalry?

6. The author says that sibling rivalry is normal. Do you agree or disagree?

7. What are some of the positive aspects of sibling rivalry?

8. How well do you manage sibling rivalry in your home now? Rate yourself on a scale of 1—10, with 10 being the best.

9. What did you discover about yourself when your were writing the letter on page four to your parents?

10. After completing this chapter, the greatest insight I received about myself was ...

CHAPTER 10

Is There Order in the House?

Our five-year-old daughter, Heidi, pulled her four-year-old sister in a little red wagon up and down the sidewalk in front of our house. A crudely lettered sign taped to the wagon said, *Kid for Sale, Cheap.*

Heidi was angry at her younger sister, Liesl, and why shouldn't she be? Her privileges as an only child had been curtailed by the intrusion of this child into the Rickerson family. Heidi now had to share the affections of her parents and relatives and the resources of the family. Her solution was to sell the kid, cheap! We have had a lot of fun with Heidi and Liesl over this incident, but there is a deep message in this story. Birth order is an important part of sibling rivalry. Some of the conflict between siblings comes from the advantages and disadvantages they experience through their position in the family. A child may believe that another child has a favored position in the family. When this happens, often the child feeling at a disadvantage will try to compensate—or become discouraged and give up.

One of the keys to managing sibling rivalry in your home is to understand the special pressures of each position and take the appropriate steps to diffuse these possibly explosive situations. In the following pages we will look at birth order and how it affects children. Some characteristics are generally associated with the order of your child's birth. Genetic factors of dominance and compliance effect birth order as well. There are exceptions, but you will probably identify with the following characteristics and behaviors of your number one, two, and three children.

Firstborn—"Looking Out for #1"

A Star Is Born

From Heidi's perspective, she had a right to be angry with Liesl. What right did this little kid have to come along and take away her position as the star of the Rickerson family? The first child resents the first brother or sister forcing themselves in.

It's no wonder our firstborn feels so strongly about his favored position. It's not a bad deal. His arrival caused unequaled joy and celebration in the family. Remember the thrill of the birth of your first child? Can you still recapture the memory of the excitement of seeing that new miracle of life? The birth of your first child will always be extra special to you. While you can still be excited about the birth of other children, the specialness of that first birth can never be duplicated.

The celebration of the birth is just a start. That only child now has the undivided attention of two doting parents, grandparents, plus an assortment of friends and relatives. On this child we pour out our attention and affection. We talk to our firstborn, coo, touch, play and in all possible ways, lavish our attention on him.

The Price of Being a Star

We also heap our expectation of the "ideal child" on our firstborn. We want him to be brilliant, charming, well-behaved, and athletic. We tend to be more anxious, discipline harsher and expect more from our first child. The firstborn, in addition to enjoying all the attention, also feels the demands that go with the position.

Firstborns usually become very sensitive to the expectations and wishes of those significant adults around them. To keep this affection, they feel that they must please. That is why firstborns are generally more sensitive to authority. Firstborns are often more serious than their brothers and sisters and also more inflexible in their beliefs.

Sharing the Stage

"The secure and favored position as only child is lost when another baby appears to claim her or his share of the scene. We are bewildered to discover that this parental attention and love, particularly from our mother, is not longer exclusively ours. And here is where sibling rivalry begins."[1] The stage in the theater of life must be shared from now on with the intruder. Rivalry will come. As much as the first and second child may love one another—as well as they may get along—the feelings of rivalry will be there. There are some ways, however, that you as a parent can help the first child adjust to his new position.

First prepare the child for the new baby. Prepare your firstborn by talking about his brother or sister. Help your child feel part of the team. Let him help fix up the baby's room. Talk about how he will be able to help when the baby comes. Reassure your child that you will still love him just as much as always and he will still be just as special to you.

When the baby arrives, let your first child help. Give your child some specific responsibilities. Let him feel needed. When people are oohing and ahhing over the new baby, be sure to direct some of the attention to your helper.

Beware of giving too much responsibility to your first child. As the children get older, it is a temptation to give the oldest child too much reponsibility. We tend to make our oldest child the "third parent" in the family. This can cause a great deal of resentment and rivalry both on the part of the oldest child and the younger children in the family. Liesl and Bridget have been quick to state their resentments over "bossy Heidi." Numerous times Janet and I have had to remind Heidi, "You are not the parent." The problem with Heidi taking the role of the third parent is that she duplicates all our mistakes as parents and then invents some of her own. Contradictory discipline, bribery, and plain old bossiness cause numerous conflicts and resentments. Liesl and Bridget work just as hard at not allowing Heidi to parent them as Heidi does at becoming the third parent. Heidi, in college, recently signed a letter to her sister, "Love from your sister and sometimes mother, Heidi."

The answer to this dilemma is balance. It is natural to ask your oldest child for a greater degree of responsibility and some supervision of the younger children. But we give them two different messages: Be a parent but not *too much* of a parent. Just remember the dangers and don't allow your child to become another parent.

Number Two Tries Harder/ Caught in the Middle

My heart goes out to the number two child. I have seen the difficult struggles of the second-born trying to carve out a niche in the family system. When there is a third child, the position of number two becomes even more difficult. A letter to Ann Landers captures some of the intense feelings of rivalry that often accompany the number two spot in the family.

Dear Ann Landers,
Please print my letter so parents will take pity on the middle child. It is absolutely the worst spot in the family. If the baby wakes up early, it's my fault. I open the fridge too much. I slam doors. I am always standing in the wrong place and never straight enough. I wear the wrong pants. My shoes never look right. The oldest kid is perfect. Mom and Dad brag about her and carry her picture in their wallets with one of the baby, who of course is adorable and very smart. In fact, he may be a genius. Next to him, I am an idiot. Please print my letter for the sake of every middle child in the world. We need your help.
—Utah Misfit[2]

The second child, caught in the middle, often has the most intense feelings of rivalry. Many times there is the "perfect" firstborn and the darling little baby. How does the middle child fight the battle for self-identity on two fronts at the same time?

The number two child must try harder. While he may start out life more peacefully than did the firstborn child (his parents are more relaxed), the secondborn soon realizes he was born into a rivalry. Perhaps this is why second-borns are often strong-willed children, often revolutionaries. They have to be assertive to get their fair share of the family resource. This is especially true if the middle child is one of three who are all the same sex. If the middle child is not the same sex as his or her siblings, then the situation changes. For example, if the first child is male, the second child a female, and the third child a male, then the middle child holds a favored position. In this case, the middle child has some definite advantages.

In some cases, the second child sees the rivalry as over-whelming and gives up. I know a family where this happened. The firstborn was a boy. The secondborn was a girl. Then came adorable twin girls. You can imagine the rest. The oldest boy received attention. The twins naturally had attention lavished on them. This left the plain little girl in the middle in a vulnerable position. Her way of handling it was to give up. She saw it was useless to compete. Because she was so quiet, the parents were not aware of what was going on. Only in later years, after much damage was done, did they find out how she really felt about her position in the family.

In our family, Heidi has played a typical older child role. She is very responsible to authority, sees herself as the "good" child and makes her sisters and us aware of that fact. Liesl, on the other hand, has faced the difficulties of being in the middle "according to the book." She is very competitive and non-conforming. That is a nice way of saying that she has been rebellious. Since the role of "perfect child" has been filled, she chose to carve her niche out in some very interesting ways. Any comparison to Heidi, no matter how innocent on our part, has been met with instant defensiveness. Liesl has shown, in many ways, that it is not easy to be a middle child in a family of all girls. Liesl and a friend who is also a middle child, after comparing notes on older siblings said, "It's not that we are so bad, it's just that Heidi and Chris are so good. It's not fair."

Easing the Pain

Your middle, or secondborn, child may never believe that his birth position is "fair," but here are some ideas on how you can ease his pain.

Keep in mind how difficult it is to be a secondborn. Extra sensititivity needs to be given the secondborn because of the unique pressures that go with his order in the family.

Beware of the oldest either subtly or not so subtly saying, "I'm the perfect child." This can be a very prideful thing on the part of the oldest child and cause deep resentment on the part of the secondborn. When you see this attitude, talk about it with your oldest child.

Let your secondborn know that he is special just the way he is. This principle is basic to just about all problems in sibling rivalry. When a child believes that his parents value his own special qualities, then he will not compete so ruthlessly with his other siblings. With this principle goes another important rule. Never compare. This only adds fuel to the rivalry.

Look for signs of sibling rivalry such as jealousy, anger, etc. Reflect back to your child what you see him *feeling*. This will help your child get in touch and deal with his own feelings.

Have open discussions of birth order issues when your child is old enough to talk about birth order in your family. We have done this several times in our family. This is another way of helping your children get a realistic picture of themselves and to understand that their feelings of sibling rivalry are natural. To help you discuss birth order with your children, there is a Family Discussion Sheet at the end of this chapter.

The Youngest Child—
Last But Not Least

No one is really sure whether being the last or the "baby" of the family is more of an advantage or a disadvantage. One thing we do know, however, is that the last is not the least. In our family, Liesl and Heidi have criticized Janet and I on how we handle Bridget. "You would never allow us to get away with that," they will say. Or, "She doesn't have to do anything compared to what we had to do at her age." There is certainly some truth in what Bridget's sisters have to say. Our discipline is not as strict as with her sisters. Maybe we know more now, or perhaps we are just tired and look in the other direction. We do tend not to expect as much in the way of work from Bridget. I'm sure, at least subconsciously, that we are trying to keep her our little girl. We struggle with the tension between independence and dependence with Bridget.

Two main issues concern the birth order of the youngest child—independence and dependence. If all goes well in the family, the youngest child can actually be more confident and *independent* than the others at a similar age. The parents are often more relaxed and confident in their parenting roles. Older brothers and sisters help teach the child. There is a danger, however, in keeping the youngest child *dependent*. This can happen in a variety of ways. If the older brothers and sisters overpower the youngest, then the "baby" of the family will follow in their shadow. If family members are always doing something *for* the youngest instead of allowing the youngest to struggle on his own, then dependence is promoted. I have seen this happen often in our family. Bridget will be slow at doing something, or not doing it to the rest of the family's expectations, and someone will jump in and do it for her. Bridget has learned to use this situation to her advantage. I really believe that she acts inadquate at times just so others will do the work for her. She enjoys the benefits of dependence, saying, "Someone will do it for me," while at the same time resenting it by saying, "You don't think I can do anything."

The youngest often strives diligently to keep up with the

older siblings. This can be an advantage and help the drive for independence, if kept in balance. If, however, the youngest child strives too hard—reaches too high—the consequences can be detrimental to their emotional growth. When Bridget was younger, we would watch her set unrealistic expectations for herself. She would want to draw as well, or make things as well as her sisters. We would try to explain to her that she was doing well *for her age*. As much as we would try to convince her that the difference in quality was a result of age, not talent, it seemed to fall on deaf ears.

The following are some suggestions to help your youngest child face his/her role in the family:

Encourage appropriate independence. Encourage independence that is reasonable for your child's age—not too high and not too low. Do not "rescue" the youngest and do for him what he can do for himself.

Examine your own feelings. Are you subconsciously wanting to keep the youngest child your "baby"?

Be careful that brothers and sisters do not set standards too high for the youngest child, or on the other hand, criticize him for lack of maturity.

As in the case of the other birth orders, *let the youngest know he is special* just the way he is.

As we have seen, each order carries its own problems. A real key to helping your children adjust to their birth order is your sensitivity to the special pressures that each position carries with it and your capacity to see each child as special and unique.

----

[1]Helene S. Arnstein, *Brothers and Sisters, Sisters and Brothers.* New York: E.P. Dutton, 1979, p. 90.

[2]Ann Landers, quoted from *The Napa Register*, July 1, 1983.

Family Birth Order
Discussion Sheet

The following are some questions you can discuss as a family to see how your children feel about the birth order in your family.

1. What do you think is the best position in the family (oldest, middle, youngest)? Why?

2. Each family member write down one advantage and one disadvantage for each position (oldest, middle, youngest).

3. If you could choose to be born in a certain position in the family, which position would you choose and why?

4. Which is the most difficult position in the family and why?

5. What would you like to tell your sisters and brothers about your position that would make things easier for you?

6. What would you like to tell your parents about your position that would make things easier for you?

7. If you were raising a family and one of your children thought that they were being treated unfairly because of their birth order, what would you do?

Discussion Questions

1. How did you feel about the advantages and disadvantages of your birth order when you were growing up? Did this cause sibling rivalry?

2. Were any of your brothers and sisters affected by how they perceived their birth order in the family? How did this affect them?

3. What signs do you see that birth order is causing sibling rivalry in your home? Which child do you believe is affected most?

4. Do you feel the firstborn, secondborn, or thirdborn child has the most difficult positon in the family? Why?

5. What one insight about the oldest child did you gain that will help you in managing sibling rivalry in your home?

6. What one insight about the second or middle child did you gain that will help you in managing sibling rivalry in your home?

7. What one insight about the youngest child did you gain that will help you in managing sibling rivalry in your home?

8. Have you ever had an open discussion with your child on birth order? What was the result?

9. A key to helping children adjust to the pressures of their birth order is the parents capacity to see each child as special and unique. On a scale of 1—10, with 10 being the best, how do you rate.

10. After reading this chapter, one thing I will do is ...

CHAPTER 11

"You're Not Fair"

As parents, our values have the potential to fuel the fires of sibling rivalry or to help control them. Each of us has a set of values. The things that we feel are important constitute a value system by which we live our lives. An important part of this value system is the standard we have for our children. Each of us has an "ideal child" pictured in his mind of what he wants his child to become. For example, one parent's "ideal child" might be neat, honest, have an outgoing personality, excel academically, etc. Another parent's "ideal child" might be quiet, self-controlled, diligent in work, have athletic ability, etc. The child in the family that lives up to the parents' values or expectations can become the favored child. The child who is the farthest from the parents' concept of an "ideal child" can become the "black sheep." When the parents' emotional and (sometimes) physical resources flow to the favored child, the stage is set for rivalry and bitter feelings between siblings. Figure 11-1 will help you visualize how this occurs.

A parent's values can cause bitterness between siblings. One couple we know have two teenage daughters. The oldest is popular in school, a good student, assertive, and has a good figure. Her sister is obese, a fairly good student, average in popularity, soft-hearted, and submissive. The

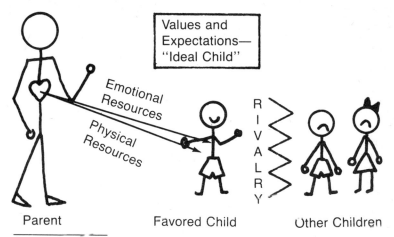

Figure 11-1. Parental Favoritism

parents value academic excellence, physical appearance, and assertiveness. They are very much into what other people think. It is not difficult to determine who is the favored child in that family. The older girl comes closest to the parents' concept of the "ideal child" and as a result is definitely favored. When conflict occurs between the sisters, the younger is usually blamed. Discipline is usually more severe for the younger daughter. The older daughter has many more photographs of herself appearing throughout the house. As a result of the parents' values, there is intense rivalry between the sisters. There is also deep bitterness that I believe will go on for many years—possibly forever.

What do you value? What qualities make up your concept of an "ideal child"? The following open-ended sentences will help you become aware of the qualities that you believe make up your "ideal child."

1. An ideal child _____ .

2. An ideal child _____ .

3. An ideal child _____ .

4. An ideal child _____ .

5. An ideal child _____ .

6. An ideal child _____ .

7. An ideal child _____ .

8. An ideal child _____ .

9. An ideal child _____ .

10. An ideal child _____ .

Now ask yourself some questions about the qualities you have just listed:

1. Which of these are Biblical qualities?

   _____

2. Do any reflect the world's values?

   _____

3. Do any qualities on your list have the potential for increasing rivalry among your children?

   _____

4. Which child in your family comes the closest to your concept of an "ideal child"?

   _____

5. Does that child receive an unequal amount of emotional and material resources because of your values?

   _____

6. Which child exhibits the least of your "ideal child" qualities?

   _____

7. Does that child feel that he/she is the "black sheep"?

   _____

What Is Favoritism?

As a Christian parent, I'm sure you are committed to not favoring one child over the other. You try to be fair. Is fairness possible? What does it mean to favor a child? First, let me give you a working definition of favoritism:

Favoritism is giving your "ideal child" a definitely unequal amount of your emotional and/or physical resources on a consistent basis while neglecting the needs of your other children.

In any family there are times when one child will clearly have more emotional or physical resources than the other children in the family. However, these resources are based upon the need of the child and the availability of the resources. This is not the kind of favoritism I am referring to in the definition. Stephen Bank and Michael Kahn, in their book, *The Sibling Bond,* said, "Favoritism occurs in all families. But in well-functioning families, children are favored for different characteristics. Or, they are favored on different days, or at different periods of their lives, so that *on the whole* no child clearly prevails."[1]

Now I would like to tread on sacred ground. *You probably like one of your children better than you do the rest.* And you probably feel quite guilty about those feelings. Let me assure you that those feelings are natural. Jesus himself had special feelings for one of his disciples: "And so she ran and came to Simon Peter, and to the other disciple whom Jesus loved" (John 20:2). We may have special feelings toward one child but that does not mean we act on those feelings and favor one child over the other. There is no indication in Scripture that Jesus favored one of His disciples. He simply enjoyed one more than the others. For what reason we do not know.

The story of Jacob and Esau, however, shows the tragedy of *acting* on special feelings for one child. Isaac and Rebekah had two sons, Jacob and Esau. Jacob became the favorite of his mother and Esau the favorite of his father. "When the boys grew up, Esau became a skillful hunter, a man of the field; but Jacob was a peaceful man, living in tents. Now Isaac loved Esau, because he had a taste for game; but Rebekah loved Jacob" (Genesis 25:27, 28). This obvious favoritism by the parents set up a bitter sibling rivalry that was not resolved for twenty years.

I do not think it is necessary for us to discuss why you might enjoy one child more than the other. There could be a variety of reasons. It is important to accept the fact and see that it does not have to lead to favoritism. However, if you have a child you are having trouble *liking,* I suggest the following: When you pray for that child, start out by thanking God for all his good qualities. List them; focus on what is good and unique in the child. *Then* pray for his weaknesses.

Fairness is making your emotional and physical resources available to each child based upon need and availability.

Let me give you an example of this definition from my own family. Liesl is an enthusiastic athlete. In the fifth grade, she fell in love with basketball. Since I have a real love for sports, I spent a lot of time teaching her the fundamentals of basketball. We went to her basketball games and made sure she had the proper equipment. We even arranged a vacation so she could attend the Washington State Basketball Camp. For quite a few years Liesl was receiving more time and physical resources than Heidi and Bridget. One day I asked Heidi if she felt Liesl was being favored. She said, "I used to think so but not any more." Heidi was beginning to understand the real meaning of fairness. We had told both Heidi and Bridget that when their interests and needs required more time and resources, these would be available to them.

When Heidi went to college, she received a greater proportion of our emotional and physical resources than ever before. She had a need and we helped to meet that need.

Our goal as parents should be to treat our children with *overall* fairness. It is impossible to treat children who have different needs, interests, and temperaments exactly the same. Even if we were able to achieve this ideal, our children would still think that we were favoring one over the other. Be careful not to play the "fairness game." In this game you try to measure out exact amounts of family resources to each child. Our children have a ledger on which they keep very accurate records. Their records will always indicate that the other children are getting more. It's a trap. "You can teach your children that there is a difference between measured fairness for all and being fair to each child based on what is needed and is available to give."[2] Our children must learn that we can love differently and yet equally. We can discipline differently without being unfair. Often children perceive the difference in the way we handle them as a difference in the way we love them. Our task is to stay on a fairness course and communicate those principles to our children. Don't be dismayed when they don't understand and accuse you of being "unfair;" that is part of parenting. Someday they will understand.

Biblical Values That Help Control Sibling Rivalry

Individuality vs. "Ideal Child"

Isn't it amazing how each of our children can be so unlike one another in personality and interests? You would think that children with the same mother and father would be more alike. But God, in His infinite wisdom, initiated a plan in which each child would be a unique creation.

When we look at our children—different in temperament and unique in interest—we should praise God for His fearful and wonderful creation. God has given us *His ideal*. His ideal is like a diamond in the rough. Together, through God's Holy Spirit and as parents, we shape and polish that diamond until the fruit of the Holy Spirit shine through brilliantly.

We must remember that *our* "ideal child" often contains our own prejudices, weaknesses, and jealousies. By insisting that each child exhibit the personality traits and interests we feel are good, we create a climate for intense rivalry among our children. By cherishing each child for his unique gifts, we help him to feel special. Our children will not feel such an intense need to compete with their brothers and sisters for the "ideal child" position; each child knows that he is ideal in his own way. This means

149

—The child who is the piano player gets as much praise as the basketball star.
—The creative child who does poorly in school gets as much praise as the "good student."
—The quiet child is assured that his quietness is valued as much as the outgoing personality of another sibling.
—Each child is loved for who he is and what he is becoming.

Inner Beauty vs. Outer Beauty

We are part of a world that worships beautiful people. We only need to look at the media to be convinced of this. It is a well-known fact that the outwardly beautiful child has some advantages over the plain child. Studies show that even teachers favor the outwardly beautiful children.

God values inner beauty. A great Biblical example of this occurred when God guided the prophet Samuel to select a king for the children of Israel. Samuel "looked at Eliab and thought, 'Surely the Lord's anointed is before Him.' But the Lord said to Samuel, 'Do not look at his appearance or at the height of his stature, because I have rejected him; for God sees not as man sees, for man looks at the outward appearance, but the Lord looks at the heart'" (1 Samuel 16:6, 7).

As parents, we are no less immune to the influence of outer beauty than a prophet of God. Whether we want to admit it or not sometimes we favor, either consciously or unconsciously, the physically attractive son or daughter. It is easy to become proud of the way they look. We cannot hide this from our children; they know if we value outer beauty. This can cause pride in the outwardly beautiful child and rivalry among the children.

The answer to this problem is obvious: As parents we must show our children that we value inner beauty more than outer beauty. We can do this by discussing this Biblical precept with our children. Even more important, we can model this precept by praising the beautiful inner qualities that we see in our children and in other people. Galatians 5:22, 23 gives us a great list of inner beauty qualities to start with: "The fruit of the Spirit is love, joy, peace, patience, kindness, goodness, faithfulness, gentleness, self-control."

Servanthood vs. Competition

Competition is the American way of life. Our nation competes to be the strongest and most productive in the world. We compete in sports, in our jobs, and, it seems, in almost all aspects of our lives. We throw our children into competition early in life, for excellence and achievement in all areas that are important to us, like Little League, school, etc.

This highly competitive spirit has a way of pitting siblings against one another in the home. The object of competition is to win. When parents push their children to succeed, it can throw siblings into competition for their parents' conditional love; often, approval is based upon how successful the child is in an area the parent feels is important. The ultimate prize is the approval of the parents. The consequence is serious sibling rivalry within the family.

I observed the effects of this fierce competition in a family. Marylin, the mother, came out of a very competitive family. She had competed vigorously with a sister to be the best. Marylin carried this competitive spirit into her marriage, competing with her husband. Their two daughters followed their mother's modeling and engaged in fierce competition with one another. The oldest daughter, Debbie, seemed to hold the edge because of her beauty and entry into the Junior Miss competition. Both girls were 4.0 students. The result was that the daughters detested each other. There was another behind-the-scenes competition going on in this family—Marylin's sister had a daughter about the same age as Debbie. She was also a Junior Miss contestant. The sister's daughter was third runner-up and Debbie was seventh runner-up. Marylin felt defeated by her sister again.

How competitive is your family? Rate yourself on a scale of one to ten, with ten being highly competitive and one indicating very little competition. Does competition in your home encourage unhealthy rivalry between your children?

It is interesting that competition is not a Biblical value. In fact, Jesus says that one becomes great, not by competing and trying to become first, but my being a servant. James and John must have come out of a competitive family. Listen to what they asked Jesus: "And James and John, the two sons of Zebedee, came up to Him, saying to Him, 'Teacher, we want You to do for us whatever we ask of You.' And He said to them, 'What do you want Me to do for you?' And they said to Him, 'Grant that we may sit in Your glory, one on Your right, and one on Your left.'" Jesus answered them with this rebuke: "Whoever wishes to become great among you shall be your servant; and whoever wishes to be first among you shall be slave of all. For even the Son of Man did not come to be served, but to serve, and to give His life as a ransom for many" (Mark 10:35-37; 43-45).

We should emphasize *serving* one another, not *competing* with one another, in our families. Competition is focusing on ourselves. This can only cause jealousy and self-centeredness. Servanthood is focusing on God and others. This brings harmony into relationships.

This talk of servanthood in the family might seem a bit idealistic to some of you, and I understand why. Servanthood is an ideal that takes time and commitment to develop. Servanthood takes place slowly in children because they are basically selfish. We may see only glimpses of this quality in our children before they leave our homes. We can, however, model servanthood in our own lives and encourage servanthood, not competition, in the lives of our children.

Competition, in moderation, is not all bad. It's fun to compete in sports and competitive games are enjoyable; but having your ego destroyed when you lose is not fun or productive for relationships. God also wants us to use our gifts to the best of our ability. "Whatever you do, do your work heartily, as for the Lord rather than for men" (Colossians 3:23). We must teach our children to do work "heartily" in whatever they do. The purpose is to honor God, not to compete with others.

Loving God vs. Worldly Success

The greatest values we can teach our children are to love God, their neighbors (including brothers and sisters), and themselves. Jesus made the importance of these values clear: "'You shall love the Lord your God with all your heart, and with all your soul, and with all your mind.' This is the great and foremost commandment. And a second is like it, 'You shall love your neighbor as yourself.' On these two commandments depend the whole Law and the Prophets" (Matthew 22:37-39).

Jesus says that our major purpose in life is to love God. The world says the major purpose in life is success, and this leads to rivalry. Loving God leads to loving relationships with other people and a good feeling about ourselves. When loving God is the first priority in our lives, our children will learn to love God and others from our example.

Our values, as parents, are the keys that help our children deal successfully with feelings of rivalry. When we value individuality, inner beauty, servanthood, and loving God, our children have a firm foundation from which to work out their relationships with their brothers and sisters.

---

[1]Stephen P. Bank and Michael O. Kahn, *The Sibling Bond*. New York: Basic Books Inc., 1982, p. 206.

[2]Carol and Andrew Calladine, *Raising Siblings*. New York: Delacorte Press, 1979, p. 40.

Discussion Questions

1. If you did not complete the open-ended sentences on pp. 145-6, please do so now. Also answer the questions about the qualities you listed. What did you learn?

2. Do you agree or disagree with the author's definition of "favoritism"? Why? Is one of your children favored? Was there any favoritism in your family when you were growing up? If so, how did you feel about it?

3. How do you feel about the statement, "You probably like one of your children better than you do the rest"?

4. Do you agree or disagree with the author's definition of "fairness"? Why? Rate yourself on a scale of 1—10 on how fair you are with your children.

5. Have you ever been caught in the "fairness game" (pp. 148-9)? How do you handle fairness with your children?

6. Read and ponder Psalm 139. What does this chapter say to you about your children's individuality? How well do you do in accepting God's unique creation in your children?

7. Read and reflect on 1 Samuel 16:6, 7. What do these verses say to you about sibling rivalry? Is this a factor in sibling rivalry in your home?

8. Read and reflect on Mark 10:35-45. On a scale of 1—10, rate yourself in competitiveness and on servanthood. How does competition in your family effect the rivalry between your children? What changes can be made in your famiiy?

9. Read Matthew 22:36-39. How well are the three great values in the passage modeled in your home? Does there need to be improvement? In what area?

10. After reading this chapter, one thing I will do is ...

CHAPTER 12

Teaching Children to Love One Another

Is it really possible to teach our children to love one another? There is probably some doubt in the minds of you parents who have just refereed a terrible fight between your children. Some of you who witness the ongoing warfare in your family may also be more than a little skeptical of "Teaching Your Children to Love One Another." I firmly believe, however, that it is possible to teach children to love their brothers and sisters. We want to see more love shown between our children and so do they. A mother told me that in a family discussion, one of her children listed "more love from my sisters" as something she wanted. But children must be taught to love one another. First we must look at love from God's perspective and then see how children develop love.

Love From God's View

Love has been distorted in our society. One secular view of love is that it is a *feeling.* When I have strong positive feelings for you then I love you. When I do not have strong positive feelings then I do not love you. This distorted view is one of the reasons why so many marriages end in divorce today. A second distortion of love held by many today is that it is *conditional.* People think, "I will love you if you perform in a certain way. When your performance no longer meets up to my expectations, then I will no longer love you." A final misconception of love that society holds is that love is *what brings me happiness.* Many people think, "My purpose in life is to be happy, therefore, my love for you is based upon whether you bring happiness into my life."

As you can see, the world's view of love is in direct opposition to a Biblical definition. Jesus taught His disciples the true meaning of love when he said, "This is My commandment, that you love one another, just as I have loved you. Greater love has no one than this, that one lay down his life for his friends" (John 15:12, 13). The love of which Jesus is speaking is *agape* love. Agape love is self-giving love—that goes on even when the other person becomes unlovable. Agape love focuses on the needs of others.

Love is an action, a decision, and a commitment. Paul describes this kind of love in 1 Corinthians 13. "Love is patient, love is kind, and is not jealous; love does not brag and is not arrogant, does not take into account a wrong suffered, does not act unbecomingly; it does not seek its own, is not provoked, does not rejoice in unrighteousness, but rejoices with the truth; bears all things, believes all things, hopes all things, endures all things. Love never fails" (1 Corinthians 13:4-8a). This kind of love does not depend on feelings. Love from God's view depends on commitment and loving feelings will follow.

Love From a Child's View

The Christian love that I have just described is a mature kind of love. Many adults have difficulty understanding and practicing unconditional love. As adults, we spend a lifetime learning to love as God loves us. Agape love is learned slowly, often painfully, through our experiences with family, God and others.

Children do not have the capacity to love in the same

way that adults love. As I mentioned earlier, this is because of their limited concept development. Love is a precept of God, but in terms of how the mind works, it is a concept.

As parents, we must realize that we are teaching our children the particulars about love. This is the basis of what will someday blossom into full-grown love in their lives. But at the same time we must acknowledge that their limitations are due to their as stages of human development, not necessarily rebellion against God. We must realize that our children are basically self-centered. It takes mature reasoning (concept development) to put ourselves in another's place to understand how they are feeling. It takes maturity to know that I can still love you (love as a decision, commitment and action) even though I don't *feel* loving towards you at the moment.

While it is important for us to understand our children's limitations in their ability to love one another, we do not need to wait until they have mature reasoning abilities before we begin teaching them to love one another. How are they going to develop the particulars that will someday make up their concept of love? We begin by teaching our children, at a very early age, everything possible about God's love. In the very early years we teach them about love by meeting their basic needs—food, touch, safety, talk, and play. As our children grow older, we model God's love for them. They see how we love them unconditionally and are always ready to forgive them. They observe how we love others. They watch closely the kind of love that we show to our spouse. We talk to them about God's love for them and others. We confront them on how they are loving their brothers and sisters. Even though they do not understand completely, we keep the vision of *unconditional love* before them. These are the building blocks they will eventually use to love others unconditionally (1 Corinthians 13:11).

Love, the Goal of Our Instruction

I believe we can say with Paul that "the goal of our instruction is love from a pure heart and a good conscience and a sincere faith" (1 Timothy 1:5). The message of the Bible is love, God's love for us and our love for others. Throughout your child's life you will be teaching him how to be loving in three basic relationships: with God, with others, and with himself. How well our children learn these relationships will determine the quality of their Christian lives and their success as individuals.

Children need to know the following four dimensions of love if they are to succeed in loving God, others, and self.

Love Is Commitment

Love is commitment, not a temporary good feeling. We talked about this earlier but I can't emphasize enough how important it is for your children to learn this. For many years our daughters Heidi and Liesl were good friends. They *felt* good about each other. In fact, when we moved to Napa the kids at the junior high school could not believe that they were sisters. The honeymoon was over, however, when Liesl hit the start of her rebellious years in the ninth grade. While Heidi remained the "perfect firstborn," Liesl rebelled against almost everything. We saw the gap widen between Heidi and Liesl. Heidi disapproved of Liesl's actions and snitched to us on occasions. This relationship deteriorated to the point that Liesl would tell me, "I just can't stand Heidi. I don't like her. I don't want to be around her." Now if Janet and I had tried to force Liesl to "like" Heidi, of course it would not have worked. What we did talk to her about was commitment, loyalty, and family love. When Heidi went away to college things started to change. We started seeing the "like" side of love returning to the relationship. Her love (decision, commitment, actions) started appearing. Now that Liesl is married and Heidi graduated from college they are once again very close. While Liesl has not come to a point where she admits that she "likes" Heidi, her *love* (decision, commitment, and action) is showing through. She writes to her regularly, takes an interest in her activities, and sews for her.

Love Is Acceptance

It is vital to teach our children to accept their brothers and sisters. This is one of the most difficult dimensions of love for all of us. It is not difficult to accept people who agree with us, or who are like us, but it is often difficult to accept those we do not understand or whose personalities differ greatly from ours. Heidi and Liesl are opposites. Liesl is athletic, innovative, outgoing, and strong-willed. Heidi is introverted, compliant, and delights in reading—not sports. For a few years Liesl decided that Heidi's qualities were all "bad"—how could anyone like someone like Heidi? While we can read sibling rivalry into that attitude, we still need to deal with the issue of nonacceptance. Liesl was basically saying, "My personality is right, and since you do not have the qualities I value, then you are unacceptable." Janet and I spent a lot of time talking to Liesl and our other girls about how God has created each of us an unique individuals and that we must accept one another. A Scripture verse we like to use is, "Accept one another, just as Christ also accepted us to the glory of God" (Romans 15:7). We all have our strengths and weaknesses, and God accepts each born-again Christian just as he is. If God accepts us, how can we not accept others in His name?

Love Is Forgiveness

At the core of love is forgiveness. Jesus said, "And whenever you stand praying, forgive, if you have anything against anyone; so that your Father also who is in heaven may forgive you your transgressions" (Mark 11:25). How do we teach our children to forgive one another? When they are very young, they experience our forgiveness. They offend us but we are always willing to forgive them. There is always a new start. They observe us forgiving others. One evening Liesl led our Family Night on forgiveness. She had been studying it in her Bible-school class. We had a good family discussion on what real forgiveness means and how difficult it is to fully forgive. We each shared some struggles we have had in forgiving certain individuals. Even though Janet's and my forgiveness of others does not always measure up to the Biblical ideal, even though we are imperfect in our forgiveness of others, the children have seen our commitment to forgive others. It is our deepest desire to work through angry feelings and forgive deeply. We now see this teaching paying off with our children. Although they struggle, they are learning how to forgive in the spirit of Christ's teaching.

Love Is Seeing Others as More Important Than Yourself

Agape love means putting the other person first. For a child, this is an almost incomprehensible concept, because a child's world centers around himself. God's Word, however, makes it clear that real love means we must see others as more important than ourselves. Paul said, "Do nothing from selfishness or empty conceit, but with humility of mind let each of you regard one another as more important than himself; do not merely look out for your own personal interests, but also for the interests of others" (Philippians 2:3, 4). Paul tells us to have the attitude of Christ who, although God, became a servant to others.

How can we teach children who are self-centered to see others as more important than themselves? The first and most important step, once again, is our modeling. Do our children see us treat others as more important than ourselves? Do we have a servant's heart or does our world revolve around our needs and desires? If this dimension of love is alive and growing in our lives, then our children will be gradually learning, by example, to have selfless love. If the foundation is laid, by the time they become adults we should observe signs of this mature love.

In addition to modeling servanthood, we must talk about it to our children. We can discuss ways that the children can put others first. You can have Family Nights or devotions studying Biblical personalities who were servants. You can continually hold up the example of Jesus as the servant of servants. When your siblings have disagreements, you can help them look at the other's point of view. While they may often reject what you are saying, they will still be learning that it is important to put others first. Here is an important point to remember: when you teach your children about love and they do not seem to be hearing you, remember that they really are listening to what you are saying. You may not see the results for years, but the seeds you plant are definitely taking root. God's Word says,

So shall My word be which goes forth
   from My mouth;
It shall not return to Me empty,
Without accomplishing what I desire,
And without succeeding in the matter
   for which I sent it.   —*Isaiah 55:11*

Structuring the Expression of Love in Your Family

While the greatest way we can teach about love is infor-
mally, there are some benefits to structuring a time for our
family to express love to one another. Sometimes children
just need help in knowing how to express love to brothers
and sisters. Here are some activities that can help.

Compliments

This is a game that builds family friendships. Send one
person from the room; have each person write a compliment about him/her on a piece of paper. Ask the person to
return and have each family member read each compliment while the person being complimented tries to guess
who made it. Redistribute the sheets of paper and repeat
the procedure until each person has been complimented.

Secret Helpers

This is an activity that works well with younger children.
Write the name of each family member on a separate slip of
paper; fold the slips and put them in a bowl. Have each
person draw a name. He should keep this name a secret.
Each day during the following week, secret helpers are to
help the person whose name they drew without them finding out. For instance, they could shine their shoes, make
their bed, etc.

Different Ways to Say "I Love You"

During one of your family times, have each person say, "I
love you" to a family member in a different way. For example, a hug, back massage, kiss, compliment, etc.

Love notes. Perhaps you have seen the little notes that say, "I love you because ..." They are available in card shops. Make some of these available and have family members start writing notes of appreciation to others in the family. This has worked well in our family. The girls have written several love notes to one another.

What I appreciate most about ... Have each family member say one thing that they appreciate most about the other family members.

My ideal day. Have each person write on a piece of paper (you could do this orally) what he would do on an ideal day. If time, finances, age, etc., were not an obstacle, what kind of things would that person do on that day? Have each person share. Afterwards, talk about how different each person's day was. What does that have to say about differences in people? Read Romans 15:7. Discuss why God wants us to accept one another.

Spotlight. Each person, in turn, must have the family spotlight turned on him. Here's how the activity works. A family member is chosen to be spotlighted. Every other family member thinks of two questions to ask the person in the spotlight. These questions must be answered with complete honesty.

The purpose of these activities is to encourage family members to think about one another and develop the ability to share their innermost thoughts.

In my book, *Family Fun Times* (Standard Publishing, 1987), an entire chapter is given to helping families structure expressions of love in the family.

Discussion Questions

1. What is the world's definition of love? What forces in our society teach this definition?

2. Read and reflect on John 15:12, 13 and 1 Corinthians 13. Based upon these Scriptures and any others you may think of, write a definition of Christian love.

3. Summarize what you think is important to remember about the way a child views love.

4. What are the building blocks that will help our children to eventually love others unconditionally?

5. Write down how each of your children currently view love.

6. Read Matthew 22:37-40. How are you now helping your children learn to love in the three relationships that are mentioned?

7. Of the four dimensions of love (pp. 158-61), which is the most difficult for you to model for your children? Why?

8. Which dimension of love do you see each of your children needing the most?

   Child #1 _____

   Child #2 _____

   Child #3 _____

9. Review the ways the author suggests for you to structure the expression of love in your family. Can you think of some other ways?

10. After reading this chapter, one thing I will do is . . .

CHAPTER 13

Keeping Peace in the Home

Sibling rivalry is natural. Your children are going to feel some jealousy toward one another. Conflict produced by this rivalry is not all bad; much can be learned from sibling rivalry. The conflict, however, if not managed properly, can become destructive. The goal of this chapter is to help you become a positive manager of sibling rivalry in your home.

We have been talking about management for much of this book. By "manage" I mean to direct, control, or teach brothers and sisters to love one another.

Let's stop here for a minute for you to evaluate how you are doing as a manager in some of the major areas of sibling rivalry. Following are ten statements about sibling rivalry. Rate yourself on a scale of 1-10 on each statement.

                                          Poor Fair Good Ex

1. I have resolved my own feelings   1 2 3 4 5 6 7 8 9 10
   about siblings in my home when
   I was growing up.

2. I understand the affects of birth   1 2 3 4 5 6 7 8 9 10
   order on my children and am be-
   ing sensitive to each child's position.

164

3. I have an understanding of my concept of an "ideal child" and how that affects sibling rivalry in our family.   1 2 3 4 5 6 7 8 9 10

4. I help each of my children feel they have a *special* place in the family.   1 2 3 4 5 6 7 8 9 10

5. I understand *realistic* fairness and am not caught in the unrealistic "fairness trap."   1 2 3 4 5 6 7 8 9 10

6. I live out the Biblical values of individuality, inner beauty, servanthood, and loving and knowing God.   1 2 3 4 5 6 7 8 9 10

7. I am teaching my children to express their feelings lovingly and honestly.   1 2 3 4 5 6 7 8 9 10

8. I am helping my children develop correct belief systems.   1 2 3 4 5 6 7 8 9 10

9. I understand the limitations my children have in understanding and expressing mature love, however, I'm teaching them the dimensions of God's love.   1 2 3 4 5 6 7 8 9 10

10. I give adequate time and attention to each child.   1 2 3 4 5 6 7 8 9 10

What did the evaluation tell you about your management skills right now? Assessing areas of strength and weakness and your management style will help you set goals to become a positive manager of sibling rivalry in your home. There are three types of management styles. See if you can determine which style you use most of the time.

Management Styles

Overmanagement

Some parents have a tendency to step into sibling conflict too quickly. Overmanagement parents often want peace and quiet at any cost and abhor conflict. A parent who overmanages does not allow arguments. Of course, this just drives the arguments and hostilities underground. When the overmanager observes conflict, he or she steps in immediately, judges who is right and wrong and administers discipline. The children learn that not only is conflict always wrong, but when conflict does occur, they are not capable of working the problem out on their own.

Undermanagement

Parents who undermanage often ignore what is going on around them. They seem to be oblivious to the actions and underlying attitudes of their children. There is little intervention on the part of these parents. Rivalry goes unchecked with children hitting, calling names, and taking unfair advantage of one another.

Another variation of undermanagement is the parent who becomes very angry but does very little about the conflict. This parent will scream, "Will you kids stop fighting!" or will discipline the children without ever really finding out what is going on. He gives little thought to how to help his children learn to negotiate their differences with one another.

Positive Management

The positive manager learns when to step into a sibling conflict and when to allow the children to work out their own differences. The positive manager watches for the subtle behavior that is the cause of many sibling conflicts. He studies the situation before intervening. He asks himself the question, "How can I help my children learn to negotiate their differences and understand themselves in this situation?" The positive manager has rules or bottom lines on what may go on between brothers and sisters. The positive manager uses a variety of discipline methods—to fit the situation.

166

At this point you may be thinking, "This all seems pretty ideal. Who could live up to these standards?" You are correct. I am presenting an ideal. Few, if any, could consistently follow all the principles we are talking about. I present the ideal realizing that neither I nor you will ever be the perfect positive manager. If, however, you can develop *some* of these skills and attitudes and use them *some* of the time you are going to do an adequate job of managing sibling rivalry in your family. Here are some helps to becoming a positive manager of sibling rivalry in your family.

A Positive Manager

Be Aware of More Than Just Fighting

Look beyond the obvious. One evening our middle daughter, Liesl, lashed out verbally at our oldest daughter for an apparently trivial matter. I was embarrassed because this did not happen in the privacy of our home. I was tempted to jump all over Liesl for her unacceptable behavior. On further investigation, I realized that Liesl was reacting to some subtle behavior on Heidi's part. There had been some low-key comments directed toward Liesl. There had been some critical looks. Liesl had packed all that away and then exploded in an unacceptable manner. We dealt with the outburst, but we also talked to Heidi about her looks and comments that had contributed to the conflict.

In another family, the parents of two quibbling siblings had been disciplining the older brother for yelling at his younger brother. Being positive managers, however, they began to look beyond the obvious and observed that the younger brother was baiting his older brother. The younger brother realized that if he picked at his brother just enough, the more passive brother would eventually lose his cool and yell. The parents would then step in and reprimand the older brother, to the delight of the younger brother. After observing this, the parents started ignoring the hollering of the older brother. The conflict subsided as the younger brother was no longer rewarded for his devious actions.

What is happening outside the home? Sometimes a child is feeling a lot of pressure outside the home and his brothers and sisters become the scapegoats. Since the child does not feel safe expressing his frustrations and anger on the source of the irritation, he unloads on his brothers and sisters. When one of your children suddenly starts becoming hostile with brothers and sisters, look beyond your home. How is your child getting along in school? Is your child having problems with some relationships outside the home? Is your child feeling like a failure in some area? Is your child mad at *you* and using a brother or sister as a scapegoat for his anger?

How does your child feel about himself? A child who is not happy with himself will often strike out at others. Often putdowns, sarcasm, and teasing are used by the child with low self-esteem so he can feel on top. If the teasing is chronic, your sibling may feel unfavorably compared to the others, thus questioning his worth and acceptance. Some children just seem to feel more insecure than others. They question their worth in spite of your efforts to love them unconditionally, spend time with them, and treat them as a special creation of God. The only answer to this dilemma is to keep on letting your child know how special he is to you. If you are living out the four values discussed earlier, then you are giving your child the basis for positive self-esteem. He must take the responsibility for seeing himself as worthwhile in your eyes and in God's eyes. For many of us the task of feeling good about ourselves has taken numerous years and substantial effort.

Use a Variety of Methods of Discipline
A sound strategy of discipline is needed to manage sibling rivalry. Our attitude toward discipline should be positive. *Discipline* and *disciple* come from the same root word. Discipline focuses on the past. When we discipline our children we do not do something to them, but we do something *with* them that will help them mature in attitude and behavior. Following are some methods of discipline that work well with sibling conflict.

Logical consequences. Logical consequences involves structuring consequences of misbehavior that are closely associated with the action. The good thing about logical consequences is that it holds the child, not the parent, responsible for the decision. Children learn from the consequence of their poor decisions.

Here are some examples of how to use logical consequences when your children quarrel. Your four-and six-year-old children are fighting over who has been spending the most time on the swing. After trying to reason with them about taking turns, the children continue to fight. Using logical consequences you would say, "Since you don't seem to be able to take turns without fighting, then neither of you can play on the swing for one hour. We will set the timer on the stove. When it buzzes you can try taking turns again." You are giving them the responsibility for whether they use the swing or not.

Here is another example of logical consequences: Your eight- and nine-year-old daughters have been playing with Barbie dolls. Arguments grow louder and louder about who is going to be Barbie and who is going to be Dawn and who gets a date with Ken. The conflict grows beyond what you feel is reasonable. You warn the girls once, saying, "If you can't get along playing Barbie, then I am going to separate you. If the arguing goes on you must spend one hour in your rooms by yourselves."

Children in close quarters naturally get tired of each other. If the weather is bad and they have been cooped up inside for a long time, or if they are tired, children get on one another's nerves. The best remedy for this is "time out." Simply have them play alone for a while.

School-age children can be given suitable work assignments to work out their hostile feelings towards one another. When you see that your children are angry and the conflict is headed toward disaster, step in with this logical consequence: "You both are angry and out of control. It is okay to be angry but not to call each other names and hit and shove. I want you to use some of that anger for something else—I have some work for you to do." By channeling your children's angry emotions, you teach your children one way of controlling or managing their anger. You also teach them that the consequence of fighting is going to be work. Since children are not overly enthused about work, this can prove to be a real motivation to work out their differences.

For very young children, redirection is a discipline that works well. They will not necessarily connect the consequences but you will be able to manage the conflict. Redirection means to direct a child away from the activity or object that is the center of the conflict to another activity or object. For example, if the fight is over who gets the crayons, direct one of the children to another project such as making something out of play dough.

Restriction of relevant privileges. When you have sibling rivalry that cannot be handled with logical consequences, communication, or disapproval, use restriction of relevant privileges. When the children are fighting over which television program to watch and you have tried to help them negotiate, then restrict the fighting siblings from watching TV for the evening. When you have reminded your children that no name-calling is allowed and you hear a descriptive word being directed at a brother or sister, restrict their TV, bike riding, telephone, or allowance privileges for a short time.

Communication. Communication is a valuable method of discipline because we help our children think through their attitudes and actions. We use communication with all methods of discipline. Even with the very young we talk to them about the loving way to treat people and the consequences of their behavior. Young children are limited in what they are able to hear and how they respond, but it is never too early to communicate at some level.

It is also important to help your children learn to communicate with one another. Janet and I have encouraged communication between our quarreling siblings by sending them into a room and saying, "Don't come out until you have worked out your disagreement. When you are ready, let me know and you can tell me your solutions." This has worked well. Usually the girls start the time at opposite ends of the room still angry. They get tired of the inactivity and start cooling down. Eventually one of them starts the negotiation process. The result is usually a reasonable solution. The advantage to this method of discipline is that it places the responsibility for resolving the conflict on them. You are not involved in listening to, "She did this and he did that." No matter who did what, they are to work out their differences or it's going to be a long day. One of the disadvantages of this method is that the more powerful child can intimidate the other.

When your children are ready to talk about what they have worked out, you will have a chance to evaluate their conflict resolution skills and give them valuable input.

When quarreling gets too excessive, have the quarreling siblings sit down and write what they *like* about each other. This gives the children a positive focus rather than a negative one. The tension begins to melt as siblings hear about their good traits rather than being criticized.

One other communication method that works well with children is to have warring siblings make a list of likes and dislikes about one another. After the lists are complete, have siblings read them to each other. Discuss some of the dislikes. Try to get siblings to acknowledge those dislikes and see how they contribute to the problem. Children must first become aware of their problems and how they affect relationships before they can change. By writing likes and dislikes on paper, the children have to think through and organize their thoughts about each other. This approach can get beyond the angry emotions that distort negotiations and enable the siblings to think more accurately about one another. Brothers and sisters can understand themselves and their siblings better. This new awareness can lead to better relationships.

Negotiation is another aspect of communication that children can learn. Sibling rivalry would be so much easier to manage if children had some basic skills in negotiation. The problem is that to negotiate a person must be able to think of alternatives to a situation. Young children are limited in their ability to think in abstract terms and thus are unable to think of alternatives. We must suggest alternatives if they are to learn to negotiate. For example, a brother and sister might be playing with building blocks.

The sister needs one more block to finish her house so she reaches over and takes a block from the car her brother is building. The brother yells, "That's mine!" and knocks over his sister's house. Dad hears the screams and after observing what has happened, helps his daughter learn how to negotiate. "What could you have done to get the block you needed?" the father asks his daughter. "I had to take it because he wants all the blocks for himself," she answers. "What if you had asked him if you could use one of his blocks for awhile?" the father asks. "He probably wouldn't give it to me," the daughter replies. "Then you would be disappointed," the father answers, "but maybe you could have completed your house a little later."

This may seem a little advanced for small children, but they will eventually learn to negotiate if parents keep teaching the children that there is always more than one alternative to a problem.

Positive reinforcement. On those occasions when your children do get along well together, be sure to praise their efforts. Children will often repeat behavior that is rewarded. Your praise and approval is a reward they seek after. Do not be afraid to be liberal in praise of good sibling behavior.

Extinction. Learn to stay out of sibling conflict that is initiated for the purpose of getting your attention. If you fall into the trap of rewarding the bad behavior by getting involved in the conflict, it is sure to happen again.

Rules

We have four firm sibling rivalry rules in our home.
1. *No name calling.* Do not underestimate the power of words to hurt an individual.
2. *No derogatory remarks about physical appearance.* I know of a case where a girl was repeatedly referred to as "fat" by her brother. She came to believe it even though she was not overweight.
3. *No remarks about the other's intelligence.*
4. *No physical violence*—hitting, grabbing, slapping, shoving, etc.

To make these rules work they must be clearly understood by your children. There must also be consequences
for siblings who break the rules (and they will be broken).

Saying, "I'm Sorry"

Here is a dilemma I'm sure you have faced. One of your
children has offended a brother or sister and needs to apologize. The questions is, do you ask your children to say,
"I'm sorry," when they really are not *feeling* sorry? To be
consistent with some of the principles in the chapter on
feelings, I would have to say "No." But in this situation
other issues are also at stake. Children need to learn to
mend relationships to ask for and receive forgiveness. I
believe that it is legitimate to ask your children to say, "I'm
sorry," when they have offended a brother or sister. Perhaps the phrase, "I'm sorry," is not the most appropriate
response to ask of a child, but is seems to be the one we
work with most. There are specifically two times when I
think it is appropriate to ask your child to apologize to a
brother or sister. (1) When there is a clear-cut case of intent
to hurt a sibling either physically or emotionally, and (2)
when both have been wrong and need to heal the relationship.

Remember that asking a child to say, "I'm sorry," is
teaching him the value of mending a relationship. It will
help the victim recover and it will also make the offender
feel better about himself once the strong emotions have
subsided. When asking a child to apologize, give him some
time to cool off. You might say, "Tommy, I know you are not
feeling sorry right now but when you feel better I want you
to say, 'I'm sorry' to your sister. I know you really love her
and want things to be right, and saying 'I'm sorry' will
help. It would even be okay if you wrote a note to her saying you are sorry. Think about it and let me know when
you are ready."

Hope for Quibbling Siblings and You

I hope that you have caught the message of hope in this
book. Usually parents feel some guilt and inadequacy

when they read "how to" publications like this. Those feelings are normal. Conscientious parents are usually hard on themselves, but the real message I want to leave with you is that your children *are learning* to love one another. Hang in there! You will one day see your children reaching out to one another in love and it will make your years as a positive manager of siblings all worthwhile.

Discussion Questions

1. Evaluate the scores you gave yourself on the ten sibling rivalry statements on pp. 164-5.

   List three strengths:

   List three weaknesses:

2. What is your management style? How does your style affect the sibling rivalry in your home?

3. Think of an example of sibling rivalry in your home that may be caused by the subtle behavior of another child.

4. Think of a time when sibling conflict might have been caused by pressures outside your home.

5. What indications are there that some of the fighting in your family is caused by one child not feeling good about himself?

6. Think of a sibling conflict in your home. Now select a logical consequence you could use to correct the behavior.

7. How could you use restriction of privileges to manage sibling rivalry in your home?

8. Which communication idea do you think would work in your family?

9. Write four rules that *you* think are important for controlling sibling rivalry in your home.
   1.
   2.
   3.
   4.

10. As a result of this chapter, I will ...

My Personal Management Plan

My first priority in sibling rivalry mangement is _____

_____

_____ .

I will accomplish this by _____

_____ .

My second priority in sibling rivalry management is _____

_____

_____ .

I will accomplish this by _____

_____ .

My third priority in sibling rivalry management is _____

_____

_____ .

I will accomplish this by _____

_____ .

My fourth priority in sibling rivalry management is _____

_____

_____ .

I will accomplish this by _____

_____ .